Mosaic

Mosaic

A Family Memoir
Revisited

MICHAEL HOLROYD

W. W. NORTON & COMPANY
New York • London

For information about permission to reproduce selections from this book, write to
Permissions, W. W. Norton & Company, Inc., 500 Fifth Avenue, New York, NY 10110

Manufacturing by R. R. Donnelley, Harrisonburg Division

Library of Congress Cataloging-in-Publication Data
Holroyd, Michael.
Mosaic : a family memoir revisited / Michael Holroyd.
p. cm.
Originally published: London : Little, Brown, 2004.
ISBN 0-393-05273-7
1. Holroyd, Michael—Family. 2. Maidenhead (England)—Social life and customs.
3. Authors, English--20th century—Biography. 4. Biographers—Great Britain—Biography.
5. Holroyd, Michael—Childhood and youth. 6. Maidenhead (England)—Biography.
7. Family—England—Maidenhead. 8. Autobiography. I. Title.
PR6058.O47Z47 2004
920—dc22

2004015725

W. W. Norton & Company, Inc., 500 Fifth Avenue, New York, N.Y. 10110
www.wwnorton.com

W. W. Norton & Company Ltd., Castle House, 75/76 Wells Street, London W1T 3QT

1 2 3 4 5 6 7 8 9 0

For you
my readers

These fragments I have shored
against my ruins.

T. S. Eliot
The Waste Land

Contents

Acknowledgements

Among the many people to whom I am grateful for help with the research for this book are Mrs M. S. Adams, Stella Astor, Neil Austin, Michael Barber, Mark Beaumont-Thomas, Lilla Bek, Alan Bell, Anthony Blond, Peter Blond, Pearl Brewis, Carmen Callil, Peter Calvert, Honor Clerk, Sarah Constantine, Diana Dracopoli, Jack Dracopoli, Margaret Dracopoli, Patricia Ellegard, Vicki Feaver, Michael Foss, Sally Gaywood, Mariolina Gent, Myfi Heim, Ann Johnson, Jim Knowlson, Judith Landry, Murray Last, Paul Levy, Linda Lloyd Jones, T. G. Lyttelton, Andrew McCall, Clare Michell, John Michell, Betty Parsons, Eduardo Sant'Anna, Jennifer Scarf, David Shepherd, Robert Skidelsky, Hilary Spurling, David Sutton, Robin Treherne-Thomas.

I have also relied on the expertise of several local historians including Judy Collingwood, Pamela Peskett, Janet Rowarth and J. Derek Skepper, all of whom made vital contributions to my researches.

I would also like to record my thanks to libraries and institutions that have assisted me: Roy Andrews at Andrews, Gwynne and Associates; the Beverley Local Studies Library;

the British Racing Drivers Club; Geoffrey J. Crump and the Cheshire Military Museum; Mrs P. Hatfield, archivist at Eton College Library; W. J. B. Meakin and Geoffrey Grant at Grant Saw and Son; the Reference Library at Hull; the Local Studies Centre of the Kensington and Chelsea Central Library; Simon Jones, curator at the King's Regiment; Alfred and Ewart Longhurst; the National Maritime Museum; the Royal Academy of Arts; the Royal Motor Yacht Club; the Royal Society of Marine Artists; the Royal Solent Yacht Club; the Royal Thames Yacht Club; Daphne Todd, president of the Royal Society of Portrait Painters; and Trinity Hospice.

I owe much, as ever, to Sarah Johnson for deciphering my text and enabling me to present it to my publishers in legible form. At Little, Brown I must thank my editors, Richard Beswick, Caroline North and Viv Redman, and proof-reader Kate Truman for continuing this process for the benefit of readers. I would also like to thank Viv Mullett for drawing the family trees.

Finally, and most sincerely, I must pay tribute to the patience, generosity and goodwill of my wife, Margaret Drabble, without which this book would never have come into existence.

List of Illustrations

Preface

OUR FAMILIES, RIGHT OR WRONG

This is a book of surprises – at any rate it has surprised me.
Some may think it eccentric: I prefer the word original.
Initially it arose out of letters I received from readers of my
family memoir, *Basil Street Blues*, which was published in
1999. I thought of it at first as a sequel or postscript, even
as a 'postmodern interactive' work. Beginning as a requiem,
it evolved into a love story, then a detective story, finally a
book of secrets revealed: an independent companion volume
which I have composed so that anyone can follow the
narrative without having read, or remembered, the earlier
book.

What it shows, I believe, is the strange interconnectedness
of our family lives. We are often reminded that we have only
to go back a few generations to find that we are, all of us,
approximately related one to another – which is why other
people's stories, however puzzling or extreme, contain so
many echoes of our own dreams and experiences.
Nevertheless, it has been an odd experience learning from

strangers about events involving my own relations, as well as finding myself having more knowledge of some fathers and grandmothers than their own daughters or grandsons have. We live in a forest of family trees, and the branches reach out in complicated paths over unexpectedly long distances. In tracing some of these connections and involvements as far as I can, I have tried to present an anatomy of well-researched, if wayward, family history.

The characters in this book are all ordinary people. But their exploits and adventures reveal how compelling fantasies, as well as mundane facts, guide our lives. It is how a writer mixes these facts and fantasies that divides the historian from the novelist, and determines whether a book is classified as fiction or (that most mysterious category) non-fiction.

1

Illuminations from the Past

A LAST GLIMPSE OF MY FATHER

I took a postchaise to Uttoxeter, and going into market at the time of high business, uncovered my head, and stood with it bare an hour before the stall which my father had formerly used, exposed to the sneers of the standers-by and the inclemency of the weather.

Samuel Johnson

'The End.'

After three years I had finished. I had written it all after the old fashion, with a pen and paper, then sent it off to Sarah Johnson. Over many years she has made herself indispensable at this stage of a book – the only person, or so I believe, since she tells me this, who can read my writing and (which is sometimes more illegible) my typewriting. She puts it on to a disk and, after much to-ing and fro-ing, time for second or third thoughts and so on, I have the print-out before me – several copies of it. The time is now approaching for me, in the unconvincing guise of a modern technological man, to edge towards my publisher. But for myself, I believe, I have finished. It is the end. I sit back – then suddenly some words from Samuel Beckett come floating into my mind. 'Finished, it's finished, nearly finished, it must be nearly finished.' And then some more words: 'How often I have said, in my life . . .

It is the end, and it was not the end.' Yet surely this really was the end, my signing off.

I called the book *Basil Street Blues*. It was not, of course, quite the end. There would be editing, proof-reading, and then publication. For the publishers that would be the end – and for readers the beginning. But for me, its author, this felt like the end. It was the late summer of 1998, and I was free. Almost free.

As I made arrangements to deliver the typescript to my literary agent, a chieftain amongst agents, the ferociously named, mild-mannered Caradoc King, I began thinking over what I had done. Certainly I had not done anything quite like it before. This was a genuine variation on what I had spent my career doing: writing people's lives. For this time it was my own life I had written. The typescript contained over a hundred thousand words. It sat there on the table. My life.

When people say that everyone has a book in him or her, they usually mean an autobiography – in whatever form it comes: a poem, a quest, documentary, confession, film or play, roman à clef. Mine was a family memoir.

Writers are naturally protective over their powers of language. If the magic works, then these mysterious marks we put on paper and send out like messages in a bottle can affect men and women, readers we never hear or see for the most part and do not know, making them laugh or cry, feel and think. Using this ancient technology, even the dead can communicate with us. Like the fabulous garment Prospero puts on in his cell, the writer's art invades our dreams, raises sea-storms and summons kings, makes them excite or entertain us, chasten, enchant. It is a mantle, too, lending writers many disguises which, like the chameleon's ability to change colour, help us find a way through difficulties and dangers.

But we do not always know what we are doing or the effect what we do will have. I didn't even know at the beginning that I was going to write an autobiography and even now had no idea what others would make of it. When I began, I thought I was writing an essay which, following the deaths of my mother and father, might help to fill the gap they had left with some understanding of their lives, and my own. I delayed starting, strangely reluctant, but as soon as I did start I was carried along by a passionate need for those memories which rose up in me as I wrote. Usually a slow writer, this time I wrote quickly, urgently, memory coming to the aid of memory, sinking and resurfacing, as I completed a hundred thousand words and reached my parents' deaths. Then I stopped.

How accurate was my story? That it had emotional integrity I felt certain. But was it factually reliable? Reading through it, I realised that I had pieced together stretches of the narrative from tales I had been told, conversations overheard (perhaps misheard), memories with a haphazard order of events which were themselves blurred by those legends that confuse all our family histories.

So I decided to become once more the professional biographer. Like an enquiry agent who asks questions and keeps watch, and then like a fictional detective who hopes to arrive at wonderful conclusions from a jumble of miscellaneous and apparently meaningless facts, I went back to work. I checked birth, marriage and death certificates, hunted for wills and probate information, examined street directories and census returns, travelled to places my parents and grandparents had told me about, and revisited places I had known when a child. I also wrote to people I had not seen for up to fifty years, asking for their recollections.

Gradually an alternative family history began to emerge, a sadder one than I had known. I began to notice how, to compensate for disappointments, men raise their status and the importance of their occupations on passports and marriage certificates, and women lower their ages. And there were more significant discrepancies moving through every phase of life: examinations never passed, money lost, illicit marriages and illegitimacies, breakdowns, secret elopements and liaisons, inexplicable deaths.

I hold the view that the lies we tell ourselves and others, the half-truths that through repetition we almost come to believe, the very fantasies that follow us like our own shadows, become part of our actual lives. Biographers are cursed by an 'irritable reaching after fact and reason'. You have only to look at the enormous process of verification we have developed in modern times. Never has there been such a colossal apparatus got ready – such an array of scaffolding, cranes, pulleys and tackle – to raise into place, with much pomp and sometimes the trumpeting abuse of lesser scholars, one quotation, complete with its groundwork of notes to inform us who else has used it, where, and to what inferior effect. Despite all this, the best biographers, I believe, must also 'pick about the Gravel' with their subjects and come to feel that intense connection with them that Keats called 'negative capability'.

Biographers walk a tightrope between passionate involvement that lures them into sentimentality, and historical detachment with its arid wastes of information. Those who write autobiographies walk the same line, though in an opposite direction, seeking not intimacy with another past, but some perspective on their own.

What I decided to do was to combine my two narratives, fact and emotion, memory and hearsay, what had been so often spoken and what remained silent. And then I added my discoveries – of events which, though never communicated, soon forgotten and eventually unknown, still formed an undetected pattern within my family. For example, I had discovered that my great-grandmother committed suicide at the age of thirty, leaving her husband to look after their three small children. One of those children was my grandfather, in whose house at Maidenhead I had passed my own childhood. I do not think he ever knew that his mother had killed herself in such an appalling way – swallowing carbolic acid and burning internally to death. Why would you tell a four-year-old boy such a terrible thing about his mother? And not having told him at the time, it would grow increasingly difficult, even pointless, to tell him later. Certainly no rumour of this tragedy reached me, and I feel sure that my father too knew nothing of it.

Yet once I discovered this unexplained suicide, I came to see it as a symbol that spoke for three generations of my family and, by implication, women from other families too: women in the attic, women with undiagnosed neuroses, suspect and unstable and a danger to themselves, women of no importance of whom little was thought or expected, women without self-esteem or occupation outside the family, solitary women who were unmarried or who sought death in marriage. I tried to tell their stories through the story of my aunt, the only one of those women I knew. Searching back for an origin to her predicament, I ended my memoir with my great-grandmother's beautiful Book of Ferns which I had found hidden away in an attic when, during my researches, I went back to my grandfather's house in Maidenhead. Into this massive volume, which had been presented to her in the early 1870s following her wedding in India, she had sewn and pressed, with great delicacy, arrangements of Indian ferns. After her death, this ill-omened volume passed briefly to her mysteriously ill daughter, and from her on to her niece, my Aunt Yolande, who began pasting in pictures of film stars from the silent 1920s, but left its final pages blank, as if a light had suddenly been switched off.

Basil Street Blues was, metaphorically, written on those last empty pages. But only when I had sent it off to my agent and publisher did I turn to a second volume that had lain many years with the Book of Ferns behind a curtain in that attic of my grandparents' house. This was a Book of Lights, drawn and coloured by my father in the 1930s when he had been an agent in London for Lalique Glass.

It was a less imposing volume than the vast, sombre, calf-bound Book of Ferns. Its boards, some twelve by fifteen inches, were covered in a dull, slightly stained canvas, gripped at the spine by a pair of steel rings. But when I opened this rather drab, uninviting exterior, my father's lights, drawn on French grey paper or on white sheets carefully pasted in, suddenly shone forth brilliantly. There were thirty-five of them, done mainly in greens and browns and yellows, all with their notes of scale and full size, none of them exposed to daylight for over sixty years. I was dazzled. Why had I not examined this book more carefully?

Every child's progress depends on parricide – so Isaiah Berlin remarked – which is to say that we must kill off our fathers' ideas and replace them with our own. My father had greatly strengthened the stubbornness I needed to survive as a biographer by pointing me towards almost any career, however ill-fitting, rather than writing. Reluctantly abandoning his vision of me as a tea-planter in Assam (a figure, as I saw it, from a Somerset Maugham story), he insisted that, despite a glaring deficiency in mathematics, I apply myself to the sciences at school, and when this petered out, he had me articled to a firm of solicitors where I languished for a year or two. Eventually, with a gesture of despair over my chronic lack of success, he recommended that I join the regular army and dig in for my old-age pension. But at this point I rebelled.

The reason, I fancy, he set me stumbling over such a steep and unnecessary obstacle course was that his own life when young had appeared so deceptively easy – only to become impossibly difficult after the war. He probably should have been an architect – that's where his talent lay. But it lay hidden. The closest he came to being an architect was during his last years when he worked for a series of building companies. Unfortunately, through one disaster and another, then another and again another, these companies all went out of business. Officially my father was their chief salesman. He had the reputation of being able to sell anything to anyone. But first he had, as it were, to sell whatever it was, however improbable, to himself – as he had tried to sell tea-planting, physics and mathematics, the law and a military career to me.

Over the years, in brisk succession, glass, steel, concrete, wood, bricks and mortar became magical substances in my father's imagination. They glittered and shone for him as he spoke of them, stood tall and proud as he praised their luminous virtues. Like a conjuror at a children's party, he appeared to perform miracles, amazing everyone with his eloquence. But as soon as he stopped talking, the light seemed to fade; and when he left, his audience would go into a decline, dismayed by their own credulity and, like men betrayed, resenting my father's hypnotic spell over them, his salesman's bag of tricks.

During his sixties and seventies, like a shipwrecked sailor frantically repairing a small raft in a rising storm of bankruptcy, my father would sit long into the evenings bent over his drawings. He wasn't meant to be drawing buildings, but selling them. Yet he loved plotting their contours on squared paper as if, through the sheer enthusiasm it generated, this devoted labour helped him to sell them – especially to people who sincerely, even desperately, didn't want to buy them.

Occasionally he would show me these drawings, but I never took much notice. I do remember, however, how handsome, almost palatial, some of them looked, though they were no more than extensions to golf clubhouses, modest conservatories or additional changing rooms and lavatories. Still, he derived much satisfaction, almost happiness, from drafting everything with accuracy and making it look good on the page. I know the feeling. It is, I now think, a very English characteristic, this potent combination of aesthetics and usefulness, this draftsman's contract.

It is a pity my family made such a habit, even a speciality, of misadventure. While the women seemed grounded in lives of miserable frustration, in strange maladies and unreachable loneliness, the men would float up into silver clouds of fantasy, and hang surreally suspended there. My grandfather, cutting loose from a legal career, sailed unsuccessfully into the tea business. My uncle, rather than my father, studied architecture before, finding himself miscast, he drifted vaguely into farming. My father, I suppose, was the most consistent: having studied nothing, except possibly gambling, he was optimistic about everything but ended up with nothing. We were all amateurs in an age of increasing professionalism. Innocents at home.

Yet there was a brief, bright interlude in this chaotic decline when, from the late Twenties to the late Thirties, the three of them had come together as directors of a company my grandfather founded called Breves, which was appointed the agent in Britain for Lalique Glass. Like the legendary

King Canute, standing on the very shores of bankruptcy with his two sons, my grandfather commanded the waves of recession to retreat. But 'what care these roarers for the name of king?' – let alone the name Holroyd. No matter: this happy band of Holroyds grew convinced that a spectacular business boom was about to sweep through the Thirties leading to a decade of peace and prosperity in the Forties. They seemed mesmerised, my grandfather and his two sons, by this beautiful French glass: the goblets, flower vases, car mascots, paperweights and decanters deliciously decorated with sunflowers and gorgeous peacocks, dragonflies and swallows for ever held in flight, cupids and water-nymphs eternally playing. How could anyone look into such wonderful objects and remain a pessimist?

Certainly they couldn't. My grandfather sold everything he possessed and borrowed more than he could repay in order to create a brilliant future in the West End of London. My father's own speciality in all this marvellous enterprise was glass lighting. He hoped to astonish the world with his ingenious table-lights ornamented with opalescent shells, his wall-lights with their flared frames of frosted or tinted glass, and his hanging lights which were sometimes constructed from inverted fruit bowls suspended from the ceiling by ropes. Some of these lights were briefly installed in transatlantic liners, and others used by fashionable restaurants. Unfortunately ornamental glass was going out of fashion in the Thirties. Besides, there were catastrophic breakages when drilling this glass to the metalwork of his lights.

My father seldom spoke to me about this early period of his life. His expectations, I believe, were set too high and his disappointment grew too painful. After the war, when I got to know him, he was struggling to find other employment. Almost anything would do. But the world was now a dark and hostile place, and his days and nights became increasingly uncomfortable. Life, which had seemed such fun, was actually bristling with traps and obstacles, he liked to remind me, and he was eager to see that I got my own quota of difficulties over and done with as soon as possible. With my own best interests ever in mind, and using deep parental ingenuity, he marshalled these hardships, both real and imaginary, all sharp and blistering, and triumphantly presented them to me like an armful of barbed wire that I must immediately embrace. This was his fatherly duty.

I did not find it easy to feel gratitude for this intimidating gift. On the contrary, I felt irritation, anxiety, disbelief – all symptoms of a necessary rebellion that, since my father's death, has been in retreat. A change is coming over me – I feel it as I write. I sense it too every day as I sit frowning over the newspapers, glare critically at the weather, complain about radio and television programmes, raise a judicious glass of wine to my mouth (is it the *fuissé* or the *fumé*?), press furiously down on the accelerator when approaching the amber lights, or simply look in the mirror each morning and see myself beginning the serious business of shaving. As I do all these ordinary things that are second nature to me, I seem to recognise my father, and can hear his voice once again paradoxically warning me: 'I wouldn't do that, Michael, if I were you.'

But, of course, he could never advise himself in this manner or escape his own second nature. He said nothing to me when I took such little notice of his architectural drawings and I regret my indifference now. As an exercise of atonement, I look carefully through the pages of illuminated glass I have found, his glass.

This Book of Lights reveals someone I barely recognise – someone with an optimism and confidence that were fading when I got to know him, and which were altogether extinguished at the end. As I turn these pages from his youth, looking at the array of lens and beaded bowls, the feather and flared pendants, the multicoloured spheres, the Louvre lights, cylinders and cubes so much of their period which my father designed more than seventy years ago, and that do him honour now, I can see him again, an old man, bent over his drawings of brick or wooden buildings, concrete or steel. I see him through his window in the evening, see him suddenly look up as if some flickering hope momentarily touches him. Then his head goes down, and he is back at work.

2

Quiet Consummation

DEATH OF MY AUNT

The leave-taking is a very, very great source of
consolation . . . but before we part may I interest you in
our Before Need Provision Arrangements? . . . Perhaps
you think it morbid and even dangerous to give thought
to the subject?

Evelyn Waugh, *The Loved One*

Costs is the only power on earth that will ever get
anything out of it now, or will ever know it for anything
but an eyesore and a heartsore.

Charles Dickens, *Bleak House*

THOMAS. I have come to be hanged, do you hear?
TYSON. Have you filled in the necessary forms?—

Christopher Fry, *The Lady's Not For Burning*

The end came suddenly: a shock but no surprise. On Christmas Day 1998, among the buoyant bright balloons, the carols, cake and holly of the nursing home, my Aunt Yolande finally gave up, and died. Over her years there she had gone downhill very gently, hardly making any noise or movement, seldom noticing the well-intended festivities, the brisk comings and goings, the shouts and cries all around her, occasionally smiling at something but never joining in.

The nursing home telephoned me that evening and I went down a few days later when the holidays had abated. It was a blue day, sunny, clear and cold. The country appeared frozen in beauty as I drove along, sealed from reality in the warmth of my car, cheerful radio-music singing out.

I felt saddened not so much by the fact of my aunt's death as by the contemplation of her life. For the last half-dozen years or so, since her last stroke, she was largely unaware of the hospital or the nursing home, and retained few memories of the past. Occasionally I would take her some old photograph albums, but she no longer seemed to recognise anyone. The past was dying for her, even as it was coming alive for me.

She was not, however, in pain, and seldom seemed distressed except when she fell ill. Towards the end I had tried to let the doctor know that I would be happy for him to assist her in dying, if dying was inevitable – not simply by allowing her to die slowly, but by positively taking her out of unnecessary anguish, as I believe I would wish for myself, and as I knew she had done for her much-loved dogs. But this kindness could not be granted her, and since she and I had never discussed the subject of voluntary euthanasia, I did not try to insist.

I rather dreaded the business of the day. At the nursing home I was handed my aunt's meagre belongings. I could hold them in one arm: a small broken mirror, a few photos, some picture postcards and a bag full of odds and ends – a powder compact, lipstick, purse, comb, handkerchief and hairpins. 'Is this all?' I asked. It was. All that was left after more than ninety years. We agreed that her clothes could be of no use to anyone now and should be burnt. I signed a form, and we exchanged compliments on my aunt's behalf: what a very polite patient she had been – never a complaint, indeed hardly a sound, over her five or six years there.

I felt grateful for anything the nursing home offered to ease the bureaucracy of death. But some things – making the funeral arrangements with an undertaker, notifying the death with the Registrar, helping a solicitor prepare probate – you must do yourself. I had done all this for my mother and father. I was a veteran. I knew what to do. Or believed I did.

At the nursing home I was given a formal notice stating that the doctor in charge had signed a medical certificate. I presented this to the hospital where the doctor worked, and received a sealed envelope containing the medical certificate itself on which was written the cause of my aunt's death (bronchopneumonia). Adding this to the bulging file of family papers I had put together while writing my recently completed memoirs (papers which were travelling with me, my passenger on the back seat of the car), I drove on to the General Register Office at Epsom. I was supremely well-equipped, able to prove with the aid of this file that I was truly my aunt's nephew, executor of her will, next of kin; and also (should anyone ask) that she had been my father's elder sister. Among these papers was her birth certificate recording that Yolande Phyllis Holroyd was born at 29 Victoria Square, Bristol, on 22 April 1902. So she had died aged ninety-six.

'A long life,' remarked the Registrar as she quickly transferred these facts from the red certificate to a black one, birth to death. But had it, I wondered, been a happy life? I could not believe it had been. I remembered sitting beside her crippled figure only a fortnight before and thinking that no one seeing her in this condition could have guessed at her privileged beginnings.

Her first twenty-five years must have been the best, living with her two brothers in a large, comfortable, Edwardian house just outside Maidenhead, a smiling, attractive girl whom I could still see in family photographs, playing tennis, going riding, bathing and water-skiing in the south of France during the long summer holidays. I had not known her in those days, and had only recently discovered a more sombre story behind the bright surface of this family-album life. She never married, though she had been unofficially engaged, apparently, for ten years or more. The love of her life, I was told, was a dashing yachtsman and soldier called Hazlehurst. The only letters she had kept over seventy years, which I accidentally came across in the lining of an old evening bag after she moved from her flat to the nursing home, had been signed 'H'. They began as passionate love letters written mainly in the mid-1930s, and then subsided into an affectionate correspondence. But afterwards, in the Second World War, Hazlehurst was posted to Italy, and my aunt learnt that he had married a young Italian girl . . .

'And what was your aunt's occupation?' asked the Registrar. I hesitated, as she waited to type my answer on to the black form. In the years I knew her, under increasingly difficult circumstances, my aunt had simply exercised the family dogs and looked after her ageing parents. Her father, having inherited a fabulous Indian tea fortune, allowed it to leak away through cautious investments in the City and then a highly incautious liaison in the bedroom. Both her parents naturally expected Yolande to marry, yet between them they had imprisoned her in spinsterhood. How could she leave her clinging, hysterical mother after her father, at the age of fifty, picked up a young married woman in his car, set her up in Piccadilly as his mistress and did not drive back home for almost eight years? – all this while his daughter was in her twenties. And what respectable man would happily marry her after such a scandal – a scandal that had left the family almost penniless? She was stranded.

So what had been her occupation? On her birth certificate there had been space only for her father's occupation which he had given as being 'of independent means', though in later life he would, in so many ways and means, become dependent on his daughter. On her parents' marriage certificate he had written 'Gentleman' as his 'Rank or Profession', while her mother left the space blank.

I quickly shuffled through these certificates and we decided to put a dash against Yolande's occupation, as we had against her married name. We gave the nursing home as her 'usual address', and I filled in my 'qualification' as being that of 'nephew'. Then I was handed a copy of the entry. Our business was complete. I was free to go.

I went next to my aunt's bank and, brandishing the Registrar's certificate, smoothing it against the glass window, mouthing my instructions, put a stop on my aunt's account. I felt rather pleased with myself for having remembered to do this. Then I drove on again to the undertakers who, ten years before, had arranged my father's cremation.

Both my parents had been cremated. I vividly remember walking at tremendous speed, as if trying to outpace the onset of grief, from the hospital in London where I had just seen my mother die straight to the undertakers half a mile away. It was a macabre place. As I strode briskly in, setting off a bell, there was a sudden commotion. Everybody stopped doing whatever they had been doing, hushed their laughter, adjusted ties, buttoned jackets and hastened to what appeared as formal positions appropriate for the bereaved. I remember sitting down opposite an official who, leaning reverently towards me, coming very close, whispered a stream of euphemisms on his pungent breath. By contrast, I was terrifically quick and cool, dry and businesslike, a very parody of efficiency, examining my watch and my diary, coughing importantly, as we made arrangements for my mother's coffin and hearse. During these proceedings we were looked down on by two burly men in dark, shabby suits who stood with their backs to the wall, lined up like soldiers, at ease but still uneasy. They would be my mother's pallbearers. Behind the taller of them a wisp of white smoke rose gently into the air. For a moment, in my heightened state, I wondered whether he was Satan risen from the underworld. Then I realised he was holding a cigarette in one of his hands clasped behind his back. When I looked down at the desk to sign some documents, he deftly moved this cigarette to his mouth and back again out of sight. I accepted an invitation to see the Chapel of Rest into which my mother's body was soon to be moved, and the flowers gathered, before her cremation service. It was really no more than a shed in the back area given a covering of paint, and in one corner, I unhappily noticed, there stood a tin of fly spray. Then, as I drove back home, the tears suddenly came and went on coming. I sat in the car outside my home waiting for this fit of crying to cease, and when it finally did, I went indoors, apparently composed again.

My father's cremation had been better, but it had disturbed my aunt. I had a rose planted in his memory, but there was no proper grave she could visit and no gravestone identifying him. He had simply vanished. She felt empty and unsatisfied when she was taken to the Garden of Remembrance after his death. Of course his name was in the Book of Remembrance – but where exactly was he? The word 'scattered' was, to her ears, nebulous, unsatisfactory. Neither my mother nor my father had spoken against cremation, and I favoured it. But my aunt did not like the idea. It smelt of hell to her. Those flames. So, I decided, she must be buried.

We arranged at the undertakers for her interment to take place in nine days' time at the annexe or extension of St Mary's Church, some two or three hundred yards from the flat where she had lived before moving into her 'usual address' at the nursing home. I had also come to look through pretty pictures of coffins. The plain pine, the élite elm, the patriotic oak. What would best suit my aunt? Here, it was indicated, lay an opportunity for my aunt to make her final statement – a statement beyond words, something inspiring, perhaps, to encourage others. What should my aunt say? What would she want to say? She who had said so little in her last years. This was an awkward decision. There was such an extravagant choice. Would she rest easy in the Class 9 with brassed handles, polished mahogany veneer and a cover of maroon velveteen; or wait more comfortably in the heavy-style Brocklebank containing special satin drapery? Might she enjoy the Last Supper with press-panelled sides and swing-bar handles, corners patterned after Michelangelo's Renaissance works and a scene of the Last Supper depicted on the lid? I glanced hesitantly at the hermetically sealed Trojan; the Lincoln, boasting a champagne interior; the Equinox with its adjustable bed; the solid timber Provincial, featuring pleated sunburst drapery; and the Tea Rose with its delicate lilac and copper shading. Eventually I picked the simple Windsor coffin for her to lie sightless in, with its gold plastic fittings, white side sheets, frillings and pillow. My aunt had lived most of her life a few miles from Windsor, I sentimentally reminded myself, while also noting with satisfaction that this coffin was rather less expensive than many of the others.

Prices had certainly risen and the repertoire of euphemisms expanded since my grandfather's death at the beginning of the 1960s. But there was less Disneyfication than Jessica Mitford predicted in her famous book, *The American Way of Death*. I was never entertained with a 'Have a Nice Death' video, or warned about cartoon 'bugs and critters' entering receptacles that were too cheap, or told stories of lamentably inexpensive caskets that blew up from an accumulation of methane gas. I can recall no invitation being made to render my aunt's natural carbon into a gemstone. Nor was I given a caged dove to release into the sky. The funeral directors never presented themselves as belonging to an exalted class – messengers from the Beautiful Beyond. The English Way of Death still retained a Dickensian aroma, rather than having acquired the sophisticated chicanery of *Six Feet Under*.

It was now mid-afternoon and, quickly eating a

sandwich, I drove over to look at the churchyard. The name of the church was actually St Mary the Virgin, but to avoid embarrassment when speaking or writing, St Mary's rank or condition is never mentioned.

The extension of the garden cemetery, which must once have been a rough open field, perhaps belonging to a farmer, had evidently been made into a churchyard at the beginning of the Second World War. The difference between the gravestones here and in the main cemetery reflects a change in English life. A hundred or more years ago it was the custom to perpetuate men's (and to a lesser extent women's) exploits and achievements on great slabs of blistering Aberdeen granite or solid Portland stone. Ranks and titles, wealth and potency, were proudly recorded, family crests sculpted, grand pretensions conveyed by tall obelisks, cupolas and pomegranates, imposing sarcophagi, Egyptian extravaganzas and elaborate neo-classical canopies. Whole paragraphs were sometimes cut into the marble to remind us of fashionable addresses, political and military eminence, terrible battles and shipwrecks, and, failing these, even honourable employment for distinguished societies and on charitable committees. To walk two hundred yards past such notable monuments is to absorb an extraordinary narrative of imperial history. But the ground is now uneven, the bulbous urns split, the heavy slabs of stone and marble rent asunder, the very angels, horsemen, saints, crazily tilting in the silence, as if an earthquake had shaken the solid ground on which that imperial past had stood. These vast congregations of the dead, united by solitude and stretching to the horizon, are like arenas where at night old friends can steal out between the upturned roots and branches and be reunited, or battlefields for lifelong enemies to re-engage in mortal combat.

But after the Second World War, it is the domestic virtues that are more modestly celebrated: beloved wife, kindly grandfather, much-loved husband, daughter, mum and dad. No one actually dies: they are 'called to God', they 'fall asleep', they 'enter into rest' – and they live on 'for ever in our hearts', 'always in our thoughts', 'until we meet again'. But, as the writing of a family memoir has taught me, in a few years almost all of us are forgotten, and it is the indecipherable inscriptions, worn away by the weather, that tell the true story.

Walking through these ranks of stone, reading their words of farewell, I feel a surprising poignancy over the enigma of departure. Here is genuine massed sadness, like a vast chorus, but inscribed without the language to express it. And this, it seems to me, conveys very well our inability to understand life and death, our need to cover the mysterious tragedy of our condition with simple conventions. As I drove back to London, I resolved to do better for Aunt Yolande.

In the week before the funeral I opened up negotiations with the solicitor, sending him anything I imagined might be of use: the certified copy of my aunt's death, and a copy of her will; a note of the money in her bank, the addresses of the nursing home, funeral directors, Department of Social Security and tax offices – to all of which I also wrote. Everything seemed to be in order.

Then I turned my attention to the flowers. Would I like a
spray or a wreath or something more sophisticated, such as
an arrangement of blooms shaped after the hesitant outline
of Surrey, the county she was to be buried in? I chose the
wreath.

The day of the funeral opened under a brilliant blue sky
which, by midday, had turned to furious rain. I was shown
into the Chapel of Rest where my aunt's body lay, rather
grandly, on the frilled white sheets and a pillow in the
Windsor coffin which, her name plate on its mount, had been
placed on a table under a series of pink-shaded lights. I
remember thinking that this coffin was too small to have
contained the streams of red tape that had festooned and
entangled her final, quiet years. I sat there somewhat
vacantly, looking at the crimson carpet, the Regency
wallpaper, the pictures of heroic Scottish landscapes, while
the rain hammered on the roof. I was glad to be alone.
Margaret, my wife, had wanted to come, but she had not
known my aunt – indeed my aunt had known no one besides
myself in these last, lost years; no one except, in an
undifferentiated way, those who had professionally looked
after her. She had outlived her two brothers and all her
contemporaries, and, even before her first stroke, was fencing
herself off from friends. It seemed to me proper that this
isolation should be marked at the end, and that I should be
her solitary mourner.

I remember feeling grateful that the nursing home, when
writing to me, 'Mark Holroyd', a personal letter with 'sincere
condolences for all the family', had regretted being unable to

send a representative to the funeral due to 'prior commitments' (did they mean prior committals?). So I am surprised when the door of the Chapel of Rest bursts open and a rather plump young woman in black, whom I have never seen before, runs in out of the wet. She is swiftly followed by the 'funeral arranger', who introduces her to me. She has that very week joined the staff at the nursing home and, though she has not 'had the pleasure and privilege' of meeting my aunt until now, wanted to come to her funeral in order to gain work experience. At that moment the minister arrives and further introductions take place. We laugh and chat, and suddenly it seems as if we are at a cocktail party. The minister is retired, he tells us, but always happy, even in atrocious weather (he laughs and we laugh) to turn out and lend a hand. In his hand he carries an authorised edition of the Bible, a battered and creased copy, in which some passages are illumined with an orange highlighter.

I get into my car and follow the hearse from the undertakers to the churchyard, peering through the steamed-up windows between the whizzing windscreen wipers. Next to me sits the young woman in black from the nursing home. The cemetery looks swollen with water as we get out and watch the coffin being unloaded and hoisted on to the pallbearers' shoulders. We form up in military fashion – a sort of Dad's Army – raise our black umbrellas and, as I walk slowly behind the coffin along the green darkness of the pathway, I see several covered trenches dug for other new bodies, with pyramids of dark brown soggy earth beside them. What a forlorn group we must look, a sad remnant, as we pass along the track, and then

straggle diagonally across the wet grass, picking our way
cautiously between the gravestones. We are heading for a hole
on the edge of the field, covered by two wooden planks that
are lifted off as we approach. Despite the rain, a gravedigger
is at work in a corner of the field and, thinking of the First
World War, I suddenly feel an urge to hum that song the
soldiers sometimes sang on the march:

> 'The bells of hell go ting-a-ling-a-ling
> For you but not for me . . .
> O Death, where is thy sting-a-ling-a-ling
> O Grave thy victor-ee?'

Of course, I don't. But all at once I hear some humming
from the probationer beside me and, glancing across at her,
see that she is crying volubly, luxuriously, her tears mixing
with the rain, while I, apparently quite unmoved, a prey to all
sorts of unlikely, out-of-season thoughts, walk silently under
the same umbrella. Anyone seeing us must have concluded
that she is the sorrowing relative and I the bland official.

We stand by the deep watery trench, and the coffin with
my aunt's body is lowered, swaying, into it, while the
minister reads passages from one of the Epistles to the
Corinthians, from St John's Gospel and Psalm 23. They are
words of miraculous comfort, hope and confidence: 'If it
were not so, I would have told you.'

As we wander back, amiably chatting, I tell the minister
what a good choice I think he made, and hear myself
sounding as if I were reporting on a British Council reading.

Then we emerge on to the road and are in another world. I discreetly tip the minister, and it is over. But not quite over. There is a moment of embarrassment, a pause, no one liking to say that he or she looks forward to seeing me again in case it should be taken as referring to my own funeral. Silently we shake hands and go our ways.

I had been managing my aunt's affairs for fifteen years, even before I was formally granted Power of Attorney in 1985. I had sold her flat, next to the cemetery, after she finally moved into the nursing home in the mid-1990s. The £50,000 it went for became her capital, though it was very much reduced by the time of her death. I and my cousin Vicky paid irregular sums into her bank account so that they would legitimately count as gifts and not income. I was particularly pleased by what I felt to be an ingenious strategy, not realising until too late that had we allowed Aunt Yolande's capital to fall below £8,000, and even in due course below £3,000, the state would have been obliged to step in and help pay the nursing expenses. This was typical of my imperfect understanding of the maze-like benefits system.

Cousin Vicky is my Uncle Kenneth's daughter, a bright, blue-eyed, blonde girl much younger than I am, now married with two children. Her life has been very different from mine and we have few interests in common. Yet when I see her I feel an instant affinity. This is all the more surprising as I have met her only a few times in my life, and so had Aunt Yolande. But Vicky is Yolande's niece, as close a blood relation as myself, and she generously volunteered to contribute some of this quixotic financial help.

The best way of dealing with my aunt's affairs, I had resolved, was to make them as simple as possible. But simplicity is a more complex matter than I imagined. I sold her few Indian Mutiny tea shares, put an end to her small building society account, and placed everything she possessed in her bank. But the solicitor now needed evidence of those long-ago sold shares, that ancient cancelled account, to smooth away the prickly problems of probate. Searching through the large cupboard where my aunt's records, fifteen years of them, were piled up, I grew once more baffled and appalled to see how her single, straightforward life became weighed down by such a density of paperwork. It lay, like a thick geological layer covering an immensity of time, above the forms, the statistics, the charts of my parents' illnesses and deaths: my private registry, an archival incoherence of ageing papers, with their faint, sickening smell of dust and despair. How could all this have happened? And why had it needed to devour so much of what people call 'spare time'? I suppose that, in a small way, my aunt and I had strayed into that obscure world, clouded by labyrinthine 'accountability', by opaque 'transparency' and the ever-circling prevarications of 'efficiency', which blights the careers of doctors, farmers, teachers and other professions. After its benign beginnings, this inhumane bureaucracy has been engulfing us all like a monstrous organism. Conceived originally as a method of helping everyone, it has been programmed so as to prevent the cheat from benefiting, and then re-engineered so that we are all identified as potential cheats. I remember how depressed I was made to feel by a language that no ordinary person speaks, an incomprehensible totalitarian language of computer-talk and committee-speak, reinforced by the convoluted jargon of local government loquacity. It seemed as if little of what I wrote to them was 'applicable', and little they sent me made sense. I communicated in paragraphs, they sent me boxes to fill in. But my lines would not fit into their spaces. We were continually at odds. All the evidence of this non-communication I had been advised to store. I tended it gingerly, gave it quantity time.

Some weeks most of my mail was actually for and about my aunt: a voluminous puzzle of papers from the Health Centre, Twilight Nurses, Age Concern, Willing Hands and the Homecare Service; from the Residents' Association, the Citizens' Advice Bureau, the Locality Team in the Social Services Department of the Surrey County Council, and the Treasurer of the Borough Council; from the Caps Central Data Team in Room 82E of the Department of Social Security office in Newcastle-upon-Tyne, the Review Section of the Disability Unit at Blackpool, the Benefits Agency at Epsom, the Inland Revenue offices at Leicester, and something called Taxguard in Peterborough; from the solicitor in Greenwich, the estate agent in Ewell, two banks, three hospitals and eventually the nursing home. Are matters as convoluted as this, I wondered, in other countries? The people in these places were usually patient and kind, but I often felt that I was in a surreal festival of circumlocution, and that to avoid total chaos I must try to choreograph a formal dance for all these bodies: a corporate fair.

And here it all was, the awful evidence, the remnants, a

mad litter of vacuity filling my cupboard, tumbling out of it, such a macabre debris of paper trailing over the years. I picked up a small bundle and read through it. What had I got? Here I was writing to my aunt's doctor asking for a report on her medical condition following what I believed to be a small stroke while she was still living in the flat we had had adapted for 'a person with disabilities'. He replies that 'it would be extremely unethical to disclose details of her medical care to you or to anyone else without her formal permission'. But formally she has no permission to give. She is too ill and besides, with Enduring Power of Attorney, I am, for such purposes, my aunt. I remind the doctor of this and, to circumvent the ethical blockage, allow some common sense to flow, I provide him with formal permission on my aunt's behalf to speak to me. Once this topsy-turvy act is performed, the doctor is able to disclose that although all the support services including consultant geriatricians have been mobilised, my aunt's 'living circumstances are unsatisfactory'. She should be moved 'as a matter of urgency' to 'correctly structured sheltered accommodation'.

The trouble is that my aunt does not want to move. Anyone who advises her to do so is seen as a messenger of death. Against her will, she was made to leave Maidenhead following her first paralysing stroke in 1980, and has never been well afterwards. She is determined not to make the same mistake again. The doctor, gravely putting all the facts in front of me, hopes I will persuade her 'to gracefully accept them'. His split infinitive reflects a split in our understanding. I cannot persuade my aunt. No one can. And she doesn't feel in the least graceful. She clings to where she is, what she knows. But the doctor feels he has now been placed in an exposed position since I will not use my power of attorney to force my aunt to accept his advice. It is all most unprofessional and he risks being implicated in the mess. He must therefore protect himself. If there is no practical way of doing what he has recommended, he warns me, 'serious illness or death' might eventually ensue – and it will be the wrong sort of death, amateur, improper, an unstructured event. My aunt is then on the verge of her ninetieth year. I decide to follow her wishes and continue employing a private army of nurses to take care of her at home. It seems to me a question of whether she dies correctly soon or incorrectly later on.

I picked out another file from the cupboard. What was this? My aunt is now in the nursing home and I am trying to make sure she receives the financial help to which she is entitled. As I interpret it, the law says that she needs £128.65 each week. She has less than half of this coming in, and the difference is made up from Income Support. But the cost of the nursing home is approximately three times what the law says she needs to live on. The social services are not able to pay any of this until I have sold her flat. Increasingly I need the help of several organisations. One of the most difficult is Barclays Bank Taxation Service. It is not beyond them to take more than a year obtaining a small tax repayment from the Inland Revenue. When I urge them on, explaining my aunt's condition and the need for money to pay for her care, I receive an acknowledgement beginning, 'Dear Miss Holroyd' and assurances that my correspondence is receiving attention. During the financial year I am looking at, the Barclays Taxation Adviser obtains a repayment of £184.70 which is good news – it will pay for two or three days' nursing and upkeep. Unfortunately I am also advised that Barclays' fees amount to £169.40, leaving my aunt with £20.30 (an hour or two of nursing).

In order to understand how anything works, to bring it under control, to see what best I should do, I must put it on paper and make a narrative. Fearing that my aunt will soon be unable to afford tax repayments, I send a letter to the Taxation Adviser, telling him that I am writing it all up and asking whether they have any objections to my quoting Barclays' financial calculations. This provokes panic. For once I get an instant reply from the Adviser, saying that she cannot reply. Someone else will reply instead. My request is being referred to her 'immediate superior', a Senior Taxation Officer. In due course he writes to explain that the matter must be put before Barclays Marketing Department. But I am not seeking to promote the business of the bank, I answer, I am trying to manage my aunt's welfare, and have merely notified the bank out of politeness. By way of reply, the Senior Taxation Adviser incomprehensibly suggests that 'you develop your request at this stage . . .' A word I have not heard for many years rises in my throat: 'Gobbledegook'. And then another: 'Mumbo-jumbo'. We may no longer say them, but we are sinking in the stuff.

I flung the file down in exasperation. The essential part of my aunt's life was never touched by this abominable accumulation of forms, brochures, leaflets, letters that came from an alien world, utterly foreign to any she would have recognised. Years ago, I remembered, she used to worry about money, but long before the end she escaped into a happier world of fantasy and imagination. There was nothing of her present in this cupboard. I hated these papers, this awful masquerade of controlled caring.

But as I closed the door, a bundle of handwritten correspondence on coloured paper fell out. These are letters from Jean and Rita, who looked after her for over ten years. I glanced through them: and suddenly my Aunt Yolande was alive again.

I hope you are not worrying about your aunt. She is fighting fit. She is always laughing at me. Saturday we were out for coffee, our walk round the park to feed the ducks and shopping in her wheelchair & this man was very rude to her so she put her walking stick round his leg & down he came. She said he won't be rude to me again. Well, she laughed so much she cryed . . . She sends her love.

That was towards the end of 1993 when she was in her young nineties and, for brief periods on good days, full of spirit. Jean and Rita continued visiting her when, eighteen months later, following another stroke and a period in hospital, she went into the nursing home.

Miss H said that she hoped she wouldn't have to stay at the place long. But it is a lovely place and she has settled down very well. It's a long time since I've seen her so contented. She even asked for her lipstick, so is her old self once again. There was a lovely birthday tea. The staff brought in a birthday cake with candles on it, Miss H blew out the candles and made a wish, and the staff and residents all sang 'Happy Birthday'. Miss H was on very good form. I had to wake her up and she was very chatty – it was a real treat to see her so well . . .

But then:

I'm afraid her mental state has greatly deteriorated. She is talking a lot about her mother and father, and says she doesn't like Slough, tho' it's alright for shopping. She is always pleased to see me but doesn't know who I am which I find very sad. She is not capable of doing anything at all for herself and has to be fed. They had roast beef for lunch so I fed her. She has to be encouraged to eat or she forgets what to do with it. Not wearing her dentures doesn't help much. I was told her mouth had shrunk and it is better to take them away altogether as she might swallow them. I take her in some odd bits and pieces now and again. She hasn't had her hair cut, but is fine in herself, clean and tidy, and looks very nice. I will always be there for her.

Here, in simple living language, is a glimpse of what may await any of us, and a sense of the reality obscured by the cloud of departmental papers that was raining upon us both, my aunt and me. Under that downpour she was transformed from a patient and human being into a robotic consumer of health which must be perpetually checked to see if it were not being fed too much health, more health than its proper entitlement. Jean and Rita were irrelevant to them, an anecdote, never a meaningful statistic. Yet they became, as it were, adopted by my dispersed and disunited family. Their indefatigable optimism held things together. When my aunt sits mutely in her chair, bent and bandaged, apparently seeing nothing, they describe her as being 'in the pink'; when she is almost dead, they acknowledge that she is 'off colour'. Of course they were paid. But money was merely an essential, never the motivating part of our agreement, a means and not an end – which was the continuing welfare of their friend, my aunt, Yolande. The state's irrelevance was her vital experience.

But none of this was of use to the solicitor. Though I had struggled to make my aunt's affairs agonisingly simple, probate reintroduced complications. The nursing home suddenly discovered a bill, over three years old, that had never been paid; the Benefits Agency somehow paid an extra instalment into my aunt's closed bank account after her death, and then set about the infinitely complex business of reclaiming it; a new branch of Barclays Bank, the Operations Centre at Haywards Heath, issuing sincere condolences, presented itself as if for a party; and my accountant entered the stage, asking to be put in touch, as though for a dance, with my aunt's solicitor, so that together they could begin calculating what interest would accrue at the bank after her death – interest which must now be added to my own taxable income. This, I thought, is how many people pass their working lives. It is called 'the real world'.

It was around this time that, reading through a long, obtuse and deeply unhelpful letter from her publisher, Oxford University Press, my wife Margaret suddenly looked up and exclaimed abruptly: 'I wish I were dead.' And I heard myself pitifully cry out: 'For God's sake, don't say that – I couldn't cope with the paperwork!'

All the bodies, teams, departments, bureaux, agencies and offices that I had laboriously choreographed into a stately waltz, now quickened their steps. The music changed and they began tripping over one another. Whatever documents were sent off to one of them were immediately demanded by another. There was much irritated jostling. New partners, too, joined the dance, such as the 'Recovery of Estates' at A Wing, Government Buildings, in Leeds. I had been in communication with Blackpool, Epsom, Ewell, Greenwich, Guildford, Leicester, Maidenhead, Newcastle and Peterborough, but never Leeds. What Leeds wanted were my aunt's bank statements going back three and a half years, also Inland Revenue documents, passbooks, share certificates for the same period, together with what they called other relevant 'personal details'. I entered the cupboard of papers once more and by the end of the day, dark with dust, held triumphantly in my arms everything that Leeds urgently needed. It was so gross a bundle that it could not fit into the extra-large fortified envelope they had provided.

My spirit of self-congratulation at this feat of recovery

faded when, a few weeks later, Leeds wrote to inform me that I owed them exactly £10,559.25. The calculations attached to this precise sum, this most untidy precise sum, were copious. I was urged to disregard the 'Capital Assured Tariff Income' from 28 November 1966 to 16 November 1975, and did so very willingly. Though the 'Treatment of Capital' information actually covered more than thirty years, the 'Adjudication Officer' had concentrated his attention on eight sections of the Social Security Administration Act of 1992 and identified a 'relevant change of circumstances' covering 151 weeks for 'JC 17 78 73B' (which is the code name he uses for my aunt). These figures are entered in a series of boxes on form QB16. The grand total impressively fills the final box. Over ten thousand pounds. I stare at it. I had read all the leaflets and brochures, gone through the documents, frowned over the instructions. But I had never mastered what they call 'the literature'. So what is it I am staring at?

It is, I begin to see, something to do with the sale of my aunt's flat. Could anyone have believed it remained empty, year after year? Apparently, yes. Knowing I had informed everyone of the sale, I wonder whether it is worth my returning to that infernal cupboard yet again and, like a character from Narnia, coming back with some splendid proof. But proof is useless, the solicitor explains, because we are not dealing with a question of fault, merely of fact. The fact is that my aunt's payment of £130 per week has been too much according to the computer, and the accumulated excess must be paid back at once or else it will attract interest.

Interest! What a word! I look unbelievingly at the papers. I cannot credit it – indeed it is pure debit. I write out a cheque.

But to offset this there was a small, curious bonus to balance the books. While writing *Basil Street Blues*, I discovered that after my grandfather left home in 1926 and established his young mistress, Agnes May, in Piccadilly, he made a legal settlement for the benefit of his wife and three children, which was amended in 1932 by a Supplemental Deed drafted to ease his passage back to the family. The language of these trusts and deeds is marvellously obscure to me, as comprehensible as atonal music and as different from the old street language of Jean and Rita as it is from modern government jargon. I remember, from my early days as an articled clerk, having the famous seventeenth-century jurist John Seldon's aphorism recited to me: 'Ignorance of the law excuses no man.' But he must, I thought, have had criminal law principally in mind. The reason he advanced was 'not that all men know the law, but because 'tis an excuse every man will plead'. By the twentieth century, the language of the law had grown so complex as to impose ignorance on all ordinary men and women. We are foreigners in our own country. The land is reverberating to the sound of competing languages, and becoming filled with expert interpreters – business consultants, financial advisers, internet teams, text-talk specialists, scientific popularisers, literary critics, political columnists and 'spin doctors' – translating one English language into another, trying profitably to treat layers of verbal ignorance. The impenetrability of legal language, with its sidesteps into Latin, remains one of the most formidable.

Read, for example, any small extract from my grandfather's Supplemental Deed of 1932:

> The Trustees shall hold Basil's share upon the like trust *mutatis mutandis* as are hereinbefore declared concerning Kenneth Holroyd's share as if the names of the said Kenneth Holroyd and Basil Holroyd were interchanged in paragraph (b) of this clause . . .

And so on for some six thousand words, covering three generations, over seventy years. These trusts and deeds, all signed, sealed and delivered God knows where, became part of a debtors' dance to which dismal rhythm my family was obliged to move, not least my aunt.

I needed a lawyer and a professional financial consultant at each elbow to break this legal code and understand its implications. Briefly stated, the Trust tied up sufficient capital so as to produce £2,000 a year income while my grandfather was alive and, in the event of his death, £2,500 to be divided between his widow and three children. The yield in 1932 was 4.7%, which suggested that there must have been some £50,000 capital involved (slightly more to provide £2,500, rather less for £2,000). Sensibly but not sensationally invested, following the index, taking inflation into account, such an income at the beginning of the 1930s would have come to £150,000 by the end of the century, while the capital itself should have risen over seventy years to something approaching eight million pounds. These were dizzying sums that might actually have existed had we succeeded in breaking the Trust. But by law one quarter of the original capital of a Trust would have had to be invested in 'narrow range' gilts and three quarters in 'wide range' equities. Even so, I speculated, it would surely not be unreasonable to hope for half these sums, an income of £75,000 from a capital of, say, four million. Was I on the trail of a lost family fortune? Could I track it down?

The track led me to the Brighton Branch of NatWest Investments, which brazenly changed its name during our negotiations to 'NatWest Wealth Management'. The wealth of the early 1930s had shrunk dramatically. There was no eight million pounds, not even four million pounds capital now. Over fifty years of wealth management had reduced the sum to £16,000, yielding my aunt a little over £300 gross annually – minus, of course, the NatWest management fees. This £300 or so was an annual nuisance partly because no bank, apparently, likes to communicate with any other bank (the NatWest and Barclays did not seem to be on speaking terms), and partly because though my aunt (since the death of her two brothers) was the sole beneficiary of the Trust's income, the assets did not actually belong to her and could not be traded.

Only when Yolande died, the last of her generation in the family, could the Trust be ended and the dwindling shares finally sold. Vicky and I decided to sell everything immediately before the capital was reduced further by additional wealth management. Each of us received about eight thousand pounds. For Vicky, who had never heard of my grandfather's mistress, Agnes May, and the legal complexities arising from his extended leave of absence from the family, this money came as a total surprise which repaid her for the generosity she had shown Aunt Yolande over her last years. For me, it went a long way to paying off the 'Recovery of Estates' bill from A Wing in Leeds.

At the same time I asked the NatWest to send me all other documents they held connected with the Trust. From these I can now piece together a little more of what happened. It appears that in 1941, when my parents separated, my father made me a ward of court – probably to prevent my mother carrying me off during the war to the safety of a neutral country, her own country, Sweden. I was then five years old and, as 'an infant' represented by my 'next friend', came before the Chancery Division of the High Court, the plaintiff in a case against the Holroyd Settlement trustees. I have no memory of this and probably had no knowledge of it at the time. I am like the 'infant prodigy' from *Nicholas Nickleby*, led by this legal friend into the foggy atmosphere of *Bleak House*. Or, more recently, perhaps an ingénue in one of the more extreme episodes of *Ally McBeal*.

The case came before Mr Justice Simmonds, a man famous for his prominent eyebrows and bright red face. I remember my father telling me that obituaries of eminent lawyers should generally be read in reverse, so that if a Lord Chief Justice, for example, were to be described as 'humane and witty', you could be reasonably certain that he was a keen advocate of capital punishment and a notorious bore. In *The Dictionary of National Biography*, Mr Justice Simmonds is described as having a nature that was 'essentially sensitive and compassionate' (though the contributor admits that this was 'not always apparent') and that the 'clarity and speed of his decisions' were 'ranked high, particularly in Chancery cases'.

It is difficult to recapture, among the Deeds of Appointment, the trustees' affidavits, the note on exhibits, the faded Case for Counsel's Opinion arriving from the bank the essence of that clarity now. This may partly be because, voluminous as these papers are, they are only a fraction of the entire paperwork given birth to by my infant case, the main body of which has been consumed, evacuated and discarded by the Chancery Registry at the Royal Court of Justice. Nor can anything now be located by the solicitor through whom I acted. Some notion of the speed of this case, however, may be apprehended, and by the standards of *Bleak House*, it is indeed quick. Our groping and floundering in Chancery does not appear to have lasted beyond 1945 – that is, a little over four years – by which time Simmonds had been created a life peer ('finding the serener and more intellectual atmosphere of the Lords and Privy Council much to his taste'). Soon afterwards he was appointed Lord High Chancellor of Great Britain.

I was obviously no match for him. I lost my case, or at least did not win it. Or possibly it is still pending. Who knows? As to Lord Simmonds's compassion, its results could be seen in the rapidly dwindling fortunes of my family after the war.

By the time I had worked this out, probate was completed and Aunt Yolande had settled into her grave –

which is to say the dark brown earth surrounding her coffin had settled and I could make arrangements for her tombstone. I was sent a brochure by the undertaker headed 'Timelessness. A Price List'. Fashions have changed since architects and sculptors chiselled vast unseated horses, veiled angels, upturned flambeaux, mantled urns and groups of pathetic mourners, kneeling, supine, into the living rock. I was offered instead various smaller designs: of a footballer, a rabbit, a shepherd, a marble teddy bear; there were rose and chamfered vases; granite memorials shaped with the outline of a heart or decorated with a couple of gliding swans. I went for simplicity: what was called 'The Wheeled Cross' headpiece in Nabresina natural stone on which my aunt's name and dates were cut in flush lead lettering. I was impressed by the skill and aesthetic seriousness of the stonemason of whom, I thought, the undertakers themselves were rather in awe – they appeared to tremble at the sound of his name, Mr Robert Kacmarczyk. Like Mr Joyboy, the venerated mortician and restorative genius of 'Whispering Glades' in Evelyn Waugh's *The Loved One*, who cleverly manipulates the expressions of his unresisting customers, he was an artist, recognised as such and deferred to by everyone.

I wanted to choose a short inscription in a language that, among all the Babel of tongues that had so jangled and upset my understanding as I grappled with my aunt's affairs, I had never heard; a language I did not see on any of the headstones in the churchyard, but which could now come to her rescue.

No exorciser harm thee!
  Nor no witchcraft charm thee!
Ghost unlaid forbear thee!
  Nothing ill come near thee!
Quiet consummation have;
  And renownèd be thy grave!

From this song, its lines in this third verse spoken alternately by Cymbeline's two sons, Guiderius and Arviragus, before they carry off the body of Cloten, I chose for my aunt the single line without a mark of exclamation.

3

Private Faces

A POSTBAG OF READERS' STORIES

Private faces in public places
Are wiser and nicer
Than public faces in private places.

W. H. Auden

While I was in the eye of this impenetrable language storm passing over my aunt's remains, well before its end, the proofs of my family memoir arrived. There was not very much to correct, but I became aware of several mysterious and frustrating gaps in the narrative, event-plots that I had been unable to develop as a novelist might have done because my researches had led nowhere.

Basil Street Blues was published during the early autumn of 1999 in Britain and the Commonwealth and the following spring in the United States and Canada. I awaited the reviews with a trepidation that was rather different from what I normally experience before the publication of my books. My biographical subjects have been figures whose professional careers and achievements belonged to the reading public. Critics had already formed their opinions about Lytton Strachey, Augustus John and Bernard Shaw – often strong opinions, involving their attitudes to homosexuality, promiscuity or socialism, that had been hammered into their ideologies, sometimes their very identities. Whatever I had written would initially collide, or perhaps coincide, with those opinions and, for the time being, produce little change in public opinion. In any event, though it is all too easy for biographers to grow sentimentally protective of their subjects and to aggrandise them, my biographies were not really intended to be vehicles of propaganda or promotion. They were non-fiction stories. Even when the secrets of their private lives were posthumously exposed, such public figures could largely take care of themselves.

But it was quite a different matter for my family. None of them were known to the general public, nor had they grand achievements to parade – quite the contrary. I began to wonder whether I had unwittingly presented their financial and emotional disasters as the entertainments of a travelling circus, goading my parents, and even my bewildered grandparents, through acrobatic hoops of fire, shutting them cheerily into cages with the lions. Glancing through an early finished copy of my family memoir when it came in the post, I seemed to see, clambering through its pages, a troupe of ungainly, poignant, gesticulating clowns (my own relations) whose griefs and disappointments, as they tumbled over one another, rang out in sidesplitting farce. I shut the book, shuddered and waited . . .

. . . and suddenly, as if in a dream, remembered Margaret advising me, while on a journey to the Far East, our plane being boarded by what looked like a band of cut-throat freedom fighters, that, whatever happened, however desperate, I *really must not* attempt to disarm them by reading aloud my lecture. This would only irritate everyone and lead to my being shot or flung overboard. It was a surreal memory signalling my uncertainties over the tone and attitude of my book.

But when the book was finally published and the reviews came in, I found to my relief that it had not been shot down. The critics on both sides of the Atlantic, in Ireland and Australia too, were generous, deciding that I had balanced 'high comedy and desperate sadness', as one of them wrote, and treating my researches when translated into narrative as a detective story. Perhaps there was some thankfulness too (reviewers being paid for the number of words they have to write rather than read) that I had at last come up with a book of moderate length.

Fifty years ago, I believe, many critics would have questioned the validity of writing a memoir of such extravagantly humdrum people. But then, over this period, our sense of blood snobbery has diminished. There were, it is true, one or two reviewers who fastened their attention further back on my remote and more distinguished ancestors (they occupy less than twenty pages of the book) – the great lawyer painted by Sir Joshua Reynolds, the noble patron who edited Edward Gibbon's *Memoirs*, the intrepid general who saved the Assam tea-planters from death during the Indian Mutiny, the eccentric cricket enthusiast who founded the Sheffield Shield competition in Australia – and then felt let down by the rapid decline and fall of the House of Holroyd.

But this was rare. Most readers seemed at home with the more recent past, the period belonging to their own parents, and treated the book as if it were a passport they needed to reach an exotic home from home. One critic concluded that I had 'done them proud!' and I remember feeling a surge of relief.

After the reviewers came the readers. Our sense of blood snobbery may have diminished in the twentieth century, but our fame snobbery has risen and supplanted it. How would my family weather this change? I was astonished by the quantity of letters I received. After all, none of the people in the book was famous – they were as unknown as are the characters in a novel before its publication, as unknown and, I hoped, as recognisable, like figures in a parable. With all this attention, suddenly, momentarily, I was a marvellous proper person, invited to be patron of a church, a member of a racquets club, to purchase a National Service tie, to attend an old school dinner, to speak at the Guildhall, contribute to a Long-Term Care seminar, address an adoption society. Among the more unexpected communications was an astronomical chart of amazing complexity which revealed 'several synchronicities' with a notorious bishop and gave prominence to my 'natal Dragon's Head'. I could not decide, and still cannot, whether this was vastly good or bad news.

Many of the letters I had grown used to receiving from readers of my biographies were, it seemed to me, responding to books I had not written. They would highlight points I had missed (which is to say details I had thought not worth putting in), identify misprints as scholarly symptoms of an unconscious attitude, or concentrate over several pages on a footnote here, the absence of a reference note there. One reader of my *Augustus John* felt saddened when, on the very first page, he read of Augustus's parents travelling from Haverfordwest to Tenby in 1877 without any mention of the fact they would have had to change trains at Milford Haven. A reader of my *Bernard Shaw* could not get past the first sentence in which, he felt convinced, I had given the wrong date for Shaw's death (a mistake occasioned by the fact that he had filed his own obituary of Shaw for *Time* magazine a month early). And why, a reader of my *Lytton Strachey* indignantly protested, had I failed to mention in any single chapter the role of the pancreas to which so many of our predicaments can be traced?

The letters arising from *Basil Street Blues* were less arcane and the responses more spontaneous. People, as it were, took some of my clothes and tried them on themselves – sometimes with surprising effects. On emerging from behind the beards of my biographical subjects I was occasionally stopped in the street by men of the same age as myself. These encounters were bizarre parodies of fame, unfocused happenings, moments of frank bewilderment. I made some notes of them, and now run them together.

'Hello! It's Michael Holroyd, isn't it?'

'Yes, I think it is.'

'I thought it was. I'm Paul/I'm Nicky/I'm Leonard . . .'

'Oh.'

'You haven't changed at all.'

'I haven't! Really?'

'I read your book in the library. What you wrote about Mr Bailey was spot on.'

'Remind me.'

'How he watched us all in the swimming pool at school.'

'He wasn't a major character, as I recall. And it's a long time ago. We were only ten.'

'Did you go to the reunion?'

'I must have been away, out of town, abroad . . .'

'It was a good show. Lots to drink. I never realised how many of us had become clergymen.'

'Clergymen!'

'Yes. I went to Matthew's/Mark's/Luke's memorial service the other day. Remember him? It was a very good show. Lots to eat and drink. But he'd become a Catholic, you know. Told no one. Not even his wife. What are you doing now?'

'I'm standing in the rain talking to you.'

'No, I mean what are you writing about next?'

'I'm not sure. I'm trying not to think about it.'

'I do a lot of jogging these days – since I retired. Lost tons of weight. Over twenty pounds, would you believe?'

'Extraordinary. There must have been much more of you.'

'So what's your news? What did you say you were writing?'

'Not much. Saw Leonard/Nicky/Paul round here last week. Remember him?'

'I don't think so. Was he in the clothing business?'

'Don't know.'

'I went round to his place once – if it was him – full of models. Wonderful.'

'I wish I'd kept up with him – if it was him.'

By now we are both staring frantically down the street wondering how to disengage ourselves from this vacuous embrace. Then, waving energetically towards imaginary friends, we plunge off suddenly, gratefully.

Other readers tackled my book more psychologically. One, blaming me for her nightmares, telephoned in the middle of the night to discuss them. A good many readers asked for advice with their own autobiographies and family memoirs – and sent me typescripts; one of them, like John Betjeman's, I remember, was in verse. Opinions seemed to differ as to whether I had written a tragedy or a comedy. When I gave it to my wife to read, I explained that it was a comedy – a black comedy in places; when she finished reading it she told me it was a tragedy – with some very good jokes. 'Oh, the familiar pain, the dreadful laughter,' exclaimed another writer on finishing the book. That sounded like tragedy. A novelist, hearing me read some passages on the radio about my parents' deaths, had sat crying in her car, unable to get out – until rescued by a handsome stranger in a corduroy suit. Was it, after all then, a romantic tragedy? But in the video shops, which are an index of our times, there is no category called tragedy.

Other readers had cried with laughter. 'I fell off my chair,' one of them, an actress, complained. She was not demanding damages, but wrote again the following week to report that she 'was crying so much I had to clean my glasses. Thank God for Optrex!' She went on to recommend my publisher to get some eye sponsorship for the book – a suggestion rather ahead of its time.

The travels and adventures of my book, like those of a satellite sending back signals from the unknown – momentary sightings of strangers' lives – began to fascinate me. Two people took *Basil Street Blues* on trains and missed their stations. One, in Italy, was hustled off early by his wife, embarrassed by the loudness of his guffawing. The other hurtled obliviously through Sussex on to Eastbourne – an episode that, since my great-grandmother mysteriously committed suicide while living at Eastbourne, could, I thought, be made into a compelling ghost story.

I had tried to move the narrative of *Basil Street Blues* through several gears, passing from something researched into something experienced, from history towards biography, formality to intimacy, a farce into an elegy. The most amusing piece of lit. crit. I received came from my stepdaughter, who described the book as an unusual mixture of *Cranford* and *King Lear*.

'I never knew you were so foreign,' protested Beryl Bainbridge, who went on to describe the book in a newspaper as a peculiarly English comedy: 'We must all keep a straight bat.' Somewhere between her novels on Hitler and Scott of the Antarctic, Beryl had once contemplated writing a fictional biography of me as the 'Boy Holroyd'. What a place on the bookshelf this would have been! Beryl might have released my dormant self, allowing me as 'the Boy' to hit heroic sixes and score miraculous goals, in a grand Utopia of metaphors. She would have granted me a fantastical new life, as the very Holroyd of Holroyds rather than a Holroyd permanently in waiting. I was promising material since I already possessed a rich, if resting, cast of characters: Swedish mother and French stepmother, a half-Irish, quarter-Scottish father and fully Hungarian stepfather who had, between them, bathed me in a glamorous glow at school. But none of this had distanced me from the other, more regularly derived schoolboys. Born of parents traumatised by two world wars, we were the children of a wounded generation. All of us were being educated, as one of them wrote to remind me, for a world that, by the time our education was complete, no longer existed. It was ripe territory for an imaginative takeover by Beryl.

Guided by my readers, I looked again at the dwindling fortunes of my family and began to understand how impossible it had been for the men to adapt to new circumstances, and how these new circumstances had come too late to benefit the women. My grandfather haphazardly losing his Indian fortune; my mother for ever travelling the world in search of a glamorous life beyond the horizon; my father, left by all his wives, ending up with only his dog to order around; my aunt with her failing memories of a life unlived. They were all symbols of the peculiar predicament of post-imperial Britain.

Having such varied cosmopolitan influences around me while growing up, I have never been able to see myself as exclusively English. Yet it is shamefully true that, despite my polyglot past, I speak only English. So probably Beryl was right: the book is 'English'. Certainly that was the reason advanced by publishers abroad for not translating it. Because of this, I came to treasure letters from foreign readers for whom, without benefit of translation, the book became part of an inner repertory. 'It is (from my vantage point) a remote world you are describing,' one of them wrote, explaining how, nevertheless, the tone and perspective had 'allowed me to enter it more fully than most guides'. I have kept these few letters from readers beyond the English-speaking world who felt I had been 'positively eye-opening' about England, believing that the point of translation is, within a framework of universal human nature, to make remote cultures more familiar.

Like a Pandora's Box, my book caused tremors from many buried memories. Though I believed that I had been portraying a unique group of extravagant characters, I found that they had struck a chord with all sorts and conditions of readers. 'I know just what you were saying. It all came back.' 'There were many faraway echoes of happenings in my own life and that of my parents.' 'I recognised a lot.' 'Your father would have got on well with my mother.' And so on. There were hundreds of these letters, though many of them went on to describe characters and events that were dramatically different from anything I had written. Yet I knew what they meant: we all had parallel pasts which, to avoid embarrassment or pain, had been brushed and combed into polite fictions. Reading these letters, with their curious stories branching crazily out in every direction, I felt that we all came from the same ground, and this feeling gave me unexpected pleasure – as if a sense of belonging had suddenly invaded my writerly isolation.

Some critics noted that my title, *Basil Street Blues*, was

misleading – and it is true that it landed the book in the music department of several bookstores, both in Britain and in the United States. But I had dreamt of creating something comparable to the music of the blues, the sadness sung out loud and long until the note of love breaks through. Could this word-music call up spirits from the deep? That is what I wished. For if they could reappear between the covers of my book and somehow touch other people's lives, then death itself perhaps might be less final.

'It would be nice to know any other facts that will inevitably be thrown up by readers,' a local historian wrote to me.

I hoped that a few of these new facts might fill the various gaps in the narrative I had become more aware of when correcting the proofs. In the event, while some of them were indeed to do this, others fell haphazardly elsewhere, extending the frontiers of my memoir into unfamiliar ground. Did I know that a much-feared headmaster of my school had been murdered by one of the boys after I left? This question came from a woman two of whose three husbands had been at the school. But another ex-schoolboy from those dreadful days of grey-collared sweaters and acute homesickness remembered meeting this fearsome master some years later with a sense of shock: 'I could not believe what a small, nervous, insignificant man he was, away from his patch.' The son of yet another schoolfriend wrote to thank me, after forty years, for giving him a pink elephant when he was a baby: and then to tell me that a few weeks back, 'at the worrying age of sixty-four', his father had 'died suddenly, and unexpectedly, from a massive heart attack, while reading the *Spectator*'. I had not put him into *Basil Street Blues*, though we were good friends in our late teens and early twenties. And now I remember that we once hired a boat whose steering went so catastrophically askew that we capsized most of the Henley Regatta – about which I wrote a short story in the manner of Jerome K. Jerome.

Some of these letters read like first drafts of, or simply ideas for, short stories. The novelist Rose Tremain, who lived when a child in Sloane Avenue, used to look through her bathroom window at the two big mansion blocks where my mother (between husbands) and I (during holidays) lived at one time or another and, staring up at them, at us perhaps, would speculate on 'people's lives in those flats and talk to them in my mind and invent stories about them . . . this was very important to the way I came to value and need a complex imaginative life running alongside my actual life'.

I was given some vivid glimpses of minor characters in my book (the novelist William Gerhardie wearing a protective saucepan on his head during an air raid in the war and afterwards, still wearing the saucepan, searching helplessly for it in his kitchen). But more people wrote to me about places, and how they had changed. The Links at Eastbourne, where my great-grandfather had retired, was now becoming a housing estate; the church where I paraded on Sundays in Winchester, while getting through my National Service, had been turned into a cinema; the apartment on Chelsea Embankment where I sometimes stayed with my mother and her third husband, and which was later bought by Sean

Connery, had previously been used by Hitler's ambassador in London, Von Ribbentrop, who, by the time we got there, had been executed following the Nuremberg trials. But the oddest news of all came from Matisse's biographer, Hilary Spurling, who offered some curious speculations over Picasso's biographer, John Richardson.

> The proprietor of the Basil Street Hotel – where you may or may not have been conceived – was the Rothschilds' [or Roseberys'] butler from Mentmore and uncle of John Richardson (himself the son of a Mentmore housemaid who married Sir Garnet Wolseley's piratical quartermaster, afterwards founder of the Army and Navy stores) – so young John may well have presided as bellboy over the Holroyd honeymoon.

My mother had enjoyed many honeymoons since then – more perhaps than I knew. 'How did you survive?' enquired a friend of one of her lovers. 'To have a beautiful mother who was in effect a *poule de luxe* must have been searing at times, yet you seemed to give the impression of being an acquaintance just looking on, and that Ulla's affairs had little to do with you.'

How can I account for this? 'All those years ago,' wrote Beryl Bainbridge, 'I wanted to throttle the Ulla of my memory for bouncing you about like a tennis ball.' But this was never how I felt about my mother. Because of my parents' separation and divorce when I was five or six, and the fact that I lived with my father's parents while growing up, my mother had in some degree seemed to leave me. So, although

I remained emotionally attached to her, there was also some distance between us. Did her escapades bring out my prudence, or was I attracted to her way of life? A little of both, I believe. Like her, I was to have affaires, and at one stage of my life, might have been called a 'womaniser' (or at least someone who attracted the attention of several 'manisers'). But perhaps of all my family, I most resemble my grandfather Fraser. Somewhat apprehensive, I was without the sting and excitement of aggression, a dreamer who (as the handling of my aunt's financial affairs shows) is maladroit over money. Fraser, his youth like mine 'much delayed', lived in a non-permissive age, yet after an exemplary thirty years of marriage, suddenly, aged fifty (approximately the age when I got married) drove off with a much younger woman. He retained, as I explained in *Basil Street Blues*, that special sensitivity to women of men whose mothers die early. My mother did not die early, but our separation may have produced a similar reaction – a few women have been all-important to me. I had not reflected on the possibility of such a pattern before reading this letter, which goes on to describe how the wife of one of my mother's lovers took him back after he had 'recovered his senses', helped him to keep his job, and paid off the debts he had accumulated entertaining my mother. This, like the other side of the moon, was a story that lay hidden from me, and presumably from my mother herself – a cautionary tale that appeals to my prudence more than to my romanticism.

But if, as several correspondents point out, my book reinforces the view that our patterns of behaviour are genetically programmed, I must also call in evidence from my Swedish grandmother Kaja to account for my mother and myself.

One evening the telephone rang and I heard the voice of Sacha Kardo-Sessoëff. He is a Russian sculptor, aged about ninety now, whom I had not seen for thirty-five years. Between the wars he had made an animated appearance as the youthful friend – '*beau garçon, sportif, flambeur et sans le sou, personnage séduisant*' – and a fellow emigré in the Life of the novelist Romain Gary.* He reintroduced himself on the telephone by reminding me that he taught me to swim in the south of France, where I spent several summer holidays with my mother. I remember him well: a romantic, wiry, outdoor man with a strange accent, a dark-skinned White Russian who obviously attracted my mother, or was attracted to her – it was difficult to tell which as a child. I liked him, though he didn't make much of a job teaching me to swim – I retain a tendency, very slowly, to sink – and he did not make much of a living either as a sculptor. Yet he always seemed happy.

When I went over to see him he was almost blind, the complete indoor man, an elegant art dealer, living in some luxury near Marble Arch. We sat in a sombre, comfortable room, paintings by French and Italian masters on his walls, stories of pictures by Raphael and Géricault he had discovered (he wanted an introduction to Anita Brookner). He told me how indignant he used to feel whenever my first

---

*Dominique Bona, *Romain Gary* (Mercure de France, 1987), p. 46.

stepfather, Edy Fainstain, was rude in public to my mother. He was not a chivalrous man, Edy, I was told, but a bully. He bullied women. Rising slowly, painfully, to his feet, staring back across time, Sacha declared that he sometimes felt like challenging Edy to a duel. Had they been in Russia, he would have called him out. At dawn. But thinking such a gesture might embarrass my mother (she was never an early riser), he did nothing. He regretted that silence now. Then, sitting down again, relaxing, he began speculating as to why my mother had put up with Edy's bad behaviour and, parting his hands in a gesture of despair to the room, concluded that she must have loved him. This was presented not so much as the solution to a mystery as another piece in the insoluble puzzle of why we love some people and not others.

But, he quickly added, this was not the reason why he had invited me over to see him. Did I know that my Swedish grandmother, Kaja, was the lover for a brief period of that amiable anarchist Jacques Prévert, author of *Les Enfants du Paradis*? Prévert had sometimes taken her to see Matisse and she enjoyed playing with his collages. Of course Kaja was dead now . . . He paused, then began again. Had there been anything resembling a Matisse, he asked, among Kaja's belongings? I replied that I had been told Kaja knew Picasso. 'That too,' Sacha answered. I could look for that too. Then suddenly we both laughed as if this were not actually the purpose of my visit, merely an excuse of a shy blind man to meet his swimmer again.

No one writes to me about my mother and father together.

The letters I read about my father are separate: how he came into the office one morning 'in a great panic' as he should have been meeting 'one of his wives' flying in from abroad – but he couldn't be sure 'which wife it was'. Another employee wrote of the bewilderment he caused in the office with his jokes. 'He was always looking for a dream,' she concluded. 'I was not sure whether he was ever really happy.' In *Basil Street Blues*, I described him travelling all over Britain after the war trying to revive his pre-war dreams of prosperity. What I had not known, or remembered, was that he went much further in pursuit of these dreams – as far as Australia, arriving there in 1950 and attempting to restart the agency for Lalique Glass. I think he believed that life in a younger country might bring back his youth. But he achieved this mainly through giving one of his small cousins 'my first tuition at cricket under the clothes line in our backyard' at Double Bay. As for Lalique Glass, that got nowhere and he soon returned.

But one reader, Merle Rafferty, remembers him in the great days of Lalique before the war, when he worked more lackadaisically, sometimes arriving as late as 11 a.m. at his basement office at the back of Bertorelli's Restaurant in Soho and taking robust charge of the breakages. His older brother, my Uncle Kenneth, turned up at the elegant showrooms in Basil Street far earlier – which was unfortunate since he always seemed in a terrific hurry, slamming doors in the faces of the staff as he rushed from room to room. They knew what was the trouble. 'Kenneth appeared to be ruled and regulated by a married lady who rang frequently to complain about something he had, or had not, done (the phone was very close to me). This upset him terribly and he was full of remorse, but impossibly rude . . . He was always in a state of agitation.' So, in his quieter way, was my grandfather, Fraser, as he gazed vacantly round the fabulous Lalique shop with its curved, 'invisible', front window in Bond Street. Fraser relied entirely and for everything on his secretary. She was 'a Mrs Booth, who insisted on being called "Miss". When she went on leave to have a baby, he was absolutely lost and unable to settle anything, ringing her at intervals to find out what he should be doing, and asking "How is the rising generation?" She was not long away, and I wondered what happened to the baby.'

But not even Miss Booth could save Lalique, though the amalgamation with Kosta Glass in Sweden and the American Corning Glassware, which produced glass bricks used by Frank Lloyd Wright, delayed its bankruptcy until 1939. As another correspondent summed up these twelve years: 'I don't think the Holroyds ever made a penny profit.'

Of all these stray pieces of mosaic, the most interesting comes from Ronald Stent, a German Jew whom my father, with the ingenious use of a huge glass elephant, helped to escape from Nazi Germany in 1935. He came to work in my father's basement office and most days 'we had beer and sandwiches at the local pub', he remembers.

Not long after my arrival, we were standing at the bar with other chaps where your father entertained us with corny jokes. One was about some Shylock-type, money-grubbing Yid. It hurt me badly. Once the others had gone I berated your father. 'I hope,' I said, 'that you know I have a reasonable sense of humour, but after the rampant anti-semitism now in Germany, this type of joke is for me beyond the pale.' Basil looked flummoxed. 'If it hurts you,' he replied, 'I will in future refrain, but that will only make me self-conscious and wary. Why don't you reciprocate by running my Scottish and Irish ancestry down? Tit for tat.'

In his generosity, Ronald Stent accepted this as useful advice about how to get on in English society. But it also reveals, I think, how by the mid-to-late 1930s my father was already beginning to fall behind the times. A few years before, Gustaff Renier had published a bestseller entitled *The English: Are They Human?*, a precursor to George Mikes's popular *How to be an Alien* (1946) and Stephen Potter's *One-Upmanship* (1952), which were read in exactly the amused spirit my father recommends. But when, in 1939, Wyndham Lewis brought out his book on racial stereotypes, recommending assimilation and calling it *The Jews: Are They Human?*, the joke was not funny and (despite favourable reviews in *The Times Literary Supplement* and the *Jewish Chronicle*) the book had to be withdrawn.*

When Ronald Stent joined my family in London, his

---

*In the British Library, perhaps to avoid embarrassment, Wyndham Lewis's book has been bound so that only *The Jews* can be seen on the spine, whereas on the spine of Renier's rather indifferent volume the whole title is visible.

brother, ten years younger than himself, was still at school in Berlin. One of the few concessions on transferring money out of Nazi Germany was for 'educational purposes'. Ronald went to visit a minor public school in Epping Forest where the headmaster agreed to take Gunther – on one condition. Having had some bad experiences with boys from abroad whose fathers had suddenly been unable to transfer fees, he asked for an established British citizen to guarantee the monthly payments. 'When I told your father what the problem was, he spontaneously offered to furnish such a guarantee,' Ronald Stent wrote to me.

I declined, explaining that in Nazi Germany such sudden bans on currency transfer were a real possibility. Basil had an alternative: 'Why don't you take out an insurance policy?' I had never heard of such a possibility. All you could insure as a private person on the Continent was your home, your life, and your bits and pieces. Basil phoned a cousin who was a Lloyd's underwriter: 'No problem,' he said, 'I will get you a quotation.' He 'phoned back shortly. 'Nothing doing,' he said. 'For the first time in my career I have been refused a quote. Hitler's Germany is uninsurable!'

But all was for the best in that worst of all possible worlds. Eventually, in 1940, Gunther reached the United States, where in due course he became well known as co-father of a new scientific discipline, molecular genetics, part of the circle that worked on the structure of DNA, and later editor of the critical edition (1980) of James Watson's *The Double Helix. A Personal Account of the Discovery of the Structure of DNA*. 'If I had accepted Basil's generous offer,' Ronald Stent adds, 'my brother would most likely have become an Englishman, and molecular biology would have lost one of its pioneers.'

One of the most touching letters I received came from an eighty-eight-year-old woman, once an actress, who had played opposite Owen Nares in the London production of Dodie Smith's *Call It a Day* in the mid-1930s. She was then twenty-four and he was forty-eight. 'We fell seriously in love and would have married if Owen could have been free – impossible in those days without a ruinous scandal.' She was suffering from a terminal illness and it 'is very painful' for her to write this letter, but she was moved to do so by a determination not to have her love for Owen Nares, and his for her, which had been fiercely discouraged by the theatrical entrepreneur Binkie Beaumont, obliterated from the record. So I record it here, with her maiden name, Mary Gaskell.

Owen Nares was the father of David Nares, my mother's third husband and the most eccentric of my stepfathers. Everyone, it seems, has a story to tell of David. A 'most entertaining rogue', one of her girlfriends writes to assure me; another describes how he would employ his most upper-class accent when telling low stories on the telephone ('So I told her to fuck orf'). My great friend at preparatory school when we were ten or twelve, John Mein, tells me that he came to work for my stepfather at Crawford's Advertising Agency in

73

the 1960s. 'A certain Mr Nares summoned me to report at 10 a.m.,' he wrote.

> After [I had waited] 40 minutes, in growing agitation, in ambled your stepfather, poured himself a strong drink from the boardroom bar, asked a few questions, then seemed to fall asleep. To keep things going I asked if he was related to the architect Nares who lived near my mother. He sprang to life . . . and a few minutes of social chat secured me the job.

Over the years John Mein worked at Crawford's he got to know my stepfather well.

> Fun to be with when things were going well and he was not completely drunk . . . I had some good ideas which pleased him. I noticed they always became 'his ideas' at client meetings . . .
>
> He had slicked back hair, Tuscan yellow teeth with a ghastly smile, wobbling jowls, and was very portly . . . On one flight back from Manchester there was only tea, coffee or soft drinks. 'Tell the captain that Mr David Nares would like to see him.' 'I can't, sir, he's flying the plane.' 'Then tell him to fly the bloody thing faster!' I drove him home, longing for a drink myself by this time, but he slammed the house door in my face with no farewell. The true character of the charmer.

About my stepfather's family I made a serious mistake in

my book. I wrote that, though David was listed in *Who's Who* as Owen Nares's only son, there had been another son, Geoffrey. 'He had been homosexual, was shot for "cowardice" in the war, and then obliterated from the family record.' This sentence provoked what a journalist from the *Daily Mail* described as 'a rare sighting' of Camilla Parker Bowles's father, Major Bruce Shand, who sent an indignant letter to the *Daily Telegraph*, printed under the heading 'Holroyd's "ghastly slur" on a gallant soldier'.

> Geoffrey Nares joined my regiment, the 12th Royal Lancers (Armoured Cars), in 1941, coming with us to the Middle East in the latter part of that year . . . Early in 1942, he fought a most gallant action in which his troop rescued several British prisoners, subsequently he went from strength to strength, proving a most courageous and intelligent officer, especially in the very dire circumstances that prevailed that summer.
>
> Towards its end, before El Alamein, there was a severe outbreak of a nasty disease called Sand Fly Fever. Geoffrey failed to recover from this when sent back to Cairo, where he died of a tumour on the brain. His obituary in *The Times* duly recorded that he died in active service.

In the last two paragraphs of his letter, Major Shand expressed the hope that measures could be put in hand for removing this slur from a brave soldier, his regiment and the Nares family.

How had I made such a lethal error? I had put 'cowardice' between inverted commas in order to indicate that I did not take the charge with moral seriousness, or rather that, for such a savage lack of understanding, I blamed the military authorities. But not taking the charge seriously, I did not check and find out that executions for cowardice had been discontinued after the First World War. I remember my stepfather speaking of some shocking event involving Germany in his brother's life that had led to the removal of his name from his father's entry in *Who's Who*, and this I did check and find to be true. I also knew that he had died in the war and, not believing his father would have eliminated him from the family record simply for a homosexual affaire (and not knowing of Owen Nares's thwarted love for Mary Gaskell), I presumed it had been for what was considered dishonourable conduct in the war. I conflated two stories and got both wrong. Actually Geoffrey Nares had been seduced in the late 1930s by a famous German ace tennis player, Baron Gottfried Von Cramm, a six-foot, green-eyed, blond runner-up at Wimbledon and in the United States championships, known as 'the prince charming of tennis' – hence the 'disreputable' connection with 'the enemy', which was peculiarly unfair because Von Cramm was imprisoned by the Nazis. Though charged with homosexuality, and smeared by the FBI as a Nazi, Von Cramm had in fact criticised the Third Reich and was punished for his opposition to Hitler. His life was made all the more strange by the long, unrequited devotion of Barbara Hutton, the glamorous Woolworth heiress to whom he was briefly married in the late 1950s.

I wrote at once to the *Daily Telegraph* admitting my error and at greater length to Major Shand explaining how I thought it had come about. I assured him that it would be corrected in any reprint of my book as well as in the American edition, which was then in preparation. He replied immediately, declaring that his indignation went not a frown further and saluting me for not blaming the publisher, the printer or a researcher. Then 'with some trepidation' he sent me a copy of his military memoirs *Previous Engagements* (in which Geoffrey Nares appears), inscribed 'In Memory of "The Nares Imbroglio"!'. Later I was able to respond with a copy of the purged American edition of my own book.

But not everyone was so graceful and generous as Bruce Shand, and I continued to have letters of outrage fired off at me by other correspondents that were more difficult to answer politely: for example from 'Yours truly' Major P. J. R. Waller MBE, JP, DL, who concluded: 'Introducing the issue of homosexuality is unworthy and largely irrelevant. What a dirty little turd you are.'

I was on safer ground with my own family. From India I received an invitation to visit the Assam tea gardens and see the legendary curved sword with which my great-grandfather had protected the lives of the tea-planters; from Sweden I was sent detailed corrections to my spelling; and from the United States a story about an Irish great-aunt whom I described as drowning in the Atlantic but who, in this version, reaches America, somehow acquires a title and lives in a terrific castle – eventually falling from one of its turrets to her death. In Britain I was offered an obscure twig from a family tree showing a Martha Holroyd marrying a James Drabble in 1840, and producing a banker son called James Edward Holroyd Drabble. We could have done with a banker. But most surprising of all was the discovery of a large family of cousins, some of them living nearby, of whom I had never heard. They were the descendants of my grandfather's mild-mannered brother Pat, the children of his son 'Mad Ivor' with whom, half a century ago, we had quarrelled and then dramatically parted.

'Is there anything more complex than the family?' one reader asks. 'Shakespeare's tragedies would not have existed without them.' Perhaps the most complex and tragic family story comes from cheerful Sally Anne, a cousin 'not of the whole blood', as the legal phrase puts it. Our Irish grandmothers were sisters (Corbets of County Cork), but Sally was abandoned by her mother Joyce and adopted by her Aunt Betty. 'Since Betty died I feel free to investigate and search for my Dad, whom I do not remember as I was adopted when a few months old,' she wrote to me.

I used occasionally to see Sally Anne when I was very young. Her 'mother', Betty, would sometimes invite me to parties in Maidenhead. I was terrified by these parties and much preferred seeing Sally's half-brother Dick, who occasionally came to play with me at my grandparents' house. He was the only child who visited us, and I remember picking up the rumour that he was the illegitimate son of Rex Harrison. 'At the age of 20, Joyce [their mother] met Rex in the Nag's Head, Kensington,' Sally explains in her letter.

'They went to Maidenhead for a party, got very drunk and returned to Baker Street. Joyce became pregnant and was whisked away by her sister Betty to Monte Carlo – calling herself Mrs Temple [which was her maiden name] . . . my brother is now in touch with his half-sister. They regularly meet and get on well together.'

Since none of this appears in Rex Harrison's biographies (all of which acknowledge his promiscuity, infidelities and liking for 'wayward girls'), I felt pleased to have got it right and happy to learn it turned out well. I gave Sally what information I had and a year later she reported on her progress. Things had not gone well for her, but the research was advancing and she was heartbreakingly optimistic. Her husband had died, she was alone and, having recently been operated on for breast cancer, was 'at present undergoing chemotherapy', to be followed by radium treatment. Nevertheless, despite these setbacks, she was getting ahead with her researches. Reading *Basil Street Blues* had spurred her on to find out more about her own past which grew ever more interesting to her as her future became more difficult. Her mind was fully active, the family tree growing and spreading (her great-grandfather, she discovered, had a stained-glass memorial window at Worcester Cathedral) and she was planning to write her memoirs. What memoirs they would be! I imagined them as a film scenario.

Sally Anne and Dick were brought up very respectably at Maidenhead by their churchgoing Aunt Betty who pretended to be their mother. But though all letters from their real mother, Betty's sister Joyce, were confiscated, they began to suspect, even while they were still very young, that they had been adopted. After all, they were the only two of the six children in the house who were left-handed and had blue eyes. Their classes in mathematics and a whispering knowledge of biology convinced them that six children so close in age were simply too many. Sometimes they would pester their nanny with questions – and one day she blurted out the awful truth: and was instantly dismissed. This chink of light was quickly put out and the children still kept in the dark.

 'I could not help being struck by the similarity of my mother's [Joyce's] escapades and your mother's,' Sally Anne wrote to me. After more surgery and chemotherapy, she resumed her researches and came across one of those stories that are said to be stranger than fiction.

A year after the birth of her son Dick, Joyce met a very tall gentleman called Bill at the Berkeley Hotel in London and, not wishing to have a second illegitimate child, quickly married him – Rex Harrison on this occasion taking the role, a vignette, of best man. But when Joyce became pregnant with Sally, her very tall husband Bill fled abroad to neutral Switzerland, soon afterwards petitioning her for a divorce and citing as co-respondent a shorter gentleman called John, whom Joyce later married in Jamaica, while Bill himself, with a sigh of relief, retired to Frinton-on-Sea.

The happy couple travelled to Jamaica rather hurriedly, indeed urgently, after Joyce had shot a third gentleman of undiscovered height and name who had entered her bedroom in London at dead of night – and been left for dead that very night.

Joyce's two sisters, the churchgoing Betty and a dog-trainer Sheila, pursued her to Jamaica and pleaded with her to come back to England and face the music. She would not be prosecuted, not seriously, they assured her. They had not read about this murder in the newspapers – not that they read newspapers much. But they had heard nothing on the wireless. Besides, they did not really believe her. And she did not actually believe them. But she did eventually move, for reasons unexplained (probably to end married life with her moderate-sized husband, John) to Mexico City. However, the cold winter there was not good for her bones and the rainy season played havoc with her hair – and after all what was there left now but bones and hair? Not much. So, reflecting that she might bloom again for a season in a more encouraging climate, she descended on Acapulco. And here, for a brief, improbable moment (as if to prove the validity of Sally's comparison) she encountered my mother, at that time hitched up with a Viennese manufacturer of motorbicycles. Joyce, who was somewhat older than my mother, must have been in her fifties at this stage in the plot. But she was in her *young* fifties, which is to say that she still dressed as a teenager, aided by a variety of bright wigs and persistent treatment from a plastic surgeon. She had by now spent all her money and was supported financially by her two generous and disapproving sisters, the dog-training Sheila sending her £4,000 a year, and the churchgoing Betty (who was still bringing up her son and daughter at Maidenhead) adding a further £100 a week. With this money, and occasional bonuses extracted by brilliant feats of emotional blackmail, she was able to experiment with more ingenious facelifts, purchase some new jewellery, gather a pack of poodles, and, as she grew older, more wretched and deeply alcoholic, refuse all offers of humiliating help from the International Social Security. The rented villa where she holed up during the day was primitive, and her exotic nightlife in smoke-filled piano bars and garish transvestite clubs increasingly sad. Even so, she found the opportunity to marry once more, this time to a Mexican gentleman with a long name but of dubious moral stature who turned out to have a wife and two children back in Mexico – where an order was issued commanding him never to see Joyce again.

Joyce died of pneumonia and malnutrition in the mid-1990s. 'I have no idea where she is buried,' Sally Anne wrote to me.

But she was still on the trail, adding to her life in retrospect, eager to find out whether 'I too have any half-brothers or sisters'. Nothing could stop her. She had already located a cousin in Tasmania. And despite the cancer, her husband's death, the dreadful shadow of this past about which she was determined to discover more, she was brimming with curiosity, had taken up painting and was beginning to exhibit her pictures. After another dose of chemo, 'I now feel a great deal better,' she ended her letter, which she signed with her married name, Sally Anne Hurt. But in 2002 I heard she had died of cancer.

4

Self-Seeking

THE BEGINNING, A MIDDLE AND SOME SENSE OF AN END

As I was going up the stair
I met a man who wasn't there.
He wasn't there again to-day –
I wish to God he'd go away.

Anon

'You stay hidden,' writes Margaret Forster near the end of a letter to me. She is a novelist who has written two remarkable volumes of family memoirs. So is she right? By training I had learnt to explore others through myself but by temperament I like to explore myself through others. That is what I believed I had done in *Basil Street Blues*.

All good biographies are intensely personal since they are really accounts of the relationship between a writer and the subject. But biographers also hide themselves behind their subjects, inhabiting those invisible spaces between the lines of print. Had I hidden myself behind my parents and grandparents too, while trying to fix my identity through family echoes and associations?

I do appear, of course, in my book on many pages and at many places: in my grandparents' dark house and on the margins of my schools; stumbling through the army, then starting out as a writer who gains invisibility in the belief that it is the invisible person who tells the visible world's stories. Intermittently, in this manner, I tried to tell my story. So I suddenly appear, first as a child racing up and down my grandparents' garden; then, an adolescent, sitting alone in the garage, an audience of one, listening to my secret concerts on the radiogram; and then again, as my own ghost, waking from a nightmare. There are other sightings of me too: obliged to arrest myself during National Service; and, back in civilian life, corresponding with myself in the guise of my mother and my stepfather.

All these, I now see, are images of loneliness. I am the point at which my family's failures peak and end. I exult, apparently, in failure, make a set piece of it, reserve for it my most precise irony. I am not so comfortable with success, not so sure how to present it. But I have had more success, like a mirage that vanishes as I reach it, than I ever dreamt. Being someone who has two birthdays, one for each of my parents, who could not agree on a date, I have perhaps had two chances also. 'Having two birthdays means both that you were never quite born, in the ordinary way,' the biographer Carole Angier writes to me, 'and that you were doubly born, the second time as a writer.' Perhaps that is the best answer for this ambiguity.

But can I bring these two selves, the writer and the subject, together on the page? Can I write about myself not passively as a listener or reader, an echo of others? It seems to me that, whatever I write, I reveal myself, my attitudes and preferences. So why is it so difficult to use the first person singular and centre the narrative on me?

I remember, a few years ago, the uncomfortableness of having my portrait painted. A cocoon of tiredness seemed to shut off the oxygen as the artist's concentration encircled me. When I work I lose myself by concentrating on others, and afterwards I feel revived. But, though I am doing nothing but sitting in a chair as the artist's model, it is an oddly exhausting experience, as if the current of energy is travelling in the wrong direction. I sit up, brace myself, take notice, and generally behave like an animal seeking to please. I smile. At the end I feel no eagerness to look at myself. Then, when I do look, I recognise a peculiar rictus in the glare of life.

Now I must put together a pen portrait of myself as seen by others. But how can I do this? I look down now and see my hand still writing, but little else. And if I look up to face the mirror, there is an amalgam of my parents, and their parents, staring back. What have I added to the equation? I must find a story with a beginning, a middle and some end to answer this: a story about myself.

In 1979, at the age of forty-four, I accepted an invitation to teach a couple of courses, one undergraduate, the other postgraduate, at Pennsylvania State University. I planned to combine two days a week teaching (plus half a day of preparation, marking essays etc.) with trips to those manuscript libraries in the United States which held the papers of Bernard Shaw (whose biography I was then writing). This developed into a hectic, sixteen-week programme involving over fifty flights to and from Penn State. If there's a blockbuster to be written round Pittsburg Airport, I'm your man.

I had never taught anything before, indeed never been a student at a university let alone a university abroad. But this seemed a good and practical way of paying for my research journeys – with the bonus of picking up some American culture.

I was to work in the curious-sounding Ihlseng Cottage, an incongruous small building on the large modern campus, named after its nineteenth-century owner Magnus Ihlseng, a white-bearded Norwegian, Dean of the School of Mines in the 1890s. By the 1970s the cottage had become an Institute for the Arts and Humanistic Studies whose director, the well-known indefatigable academic and versatile author Stanley Weintraub, with his wife Rodelle, a fine early-autumn rose, entertained me grandly at the university's expense when I presented myself (I was especially impressed by the dishes of meat, fish and poultry from all of which, simultaneously, as in a boy's dream, we were given copious helpings).

My initial nervousness was exacerbated when, on arrival, I was handed with an air of urgency some bulky medical insurance documents. Apparently my predecessor, a scientist who came from middle Europe, had fallen ill and, being improperly insured, did not qualify for proper treatment. The result had been a bad case – or, so I gathered – a bad case of death. In the circumstances I signed everything that was placed before me rather eagerly and, after a few questions about my teaching schedule, prepared to enter the classroom. Taking a formidable breath, squaring my shoulders and putting on an expression of authority, I marched in like (remembering my mixed ancestry) the very model of an English gentleman, a Swedish count, a Scottish laird, an Irish absentee landlord: something, at any rate, considerable and impressive. But what impression did I actually create?

'He was disappointing on all counts,' remembered one of my students. She, with most of the others, had been speculating over what this 'mysterious professor' from abroad would be like. It was generally assumed that, having come so far, I would carry round me a prevailing air of importance, would strike them all as indefinably fascinating, and be of course proper and precise in the best British tradition. Indeed, in my fashion, I had tried to meet these expectations. But as I entered, a cup of coffee in one hand and a bundle of books and tapes under my other arm, there was a murmur of dismay.

No bowler, no cane, no pipe, no distinguished beard even. No 'cheerio' or 'chap' . . . He slouched. As he sat down and back in his chair, he looked at us and ran his fingers through his already disordered hair. What a letdown!

I did not know then that most of my students, both in my undergraduate and postgraduate courses, had been dragooned into attending these classes as part of their literature requirements. They were not volunteers. A press release had been circulated round the Humanities Department making me out to be a very significant person. I was to deliver one or two special lectures. And this was not all. In the library stood two glass cases that had been importantly prepared with the credentials of my career: fellowships and prizes, favourable reviews and illustrated interviews, manuscript notes, and first editions (which were in truth less rare than second editions). Standing in front of it all later that day, I felt intimidated by this glittering array. Obviously it was the living embodiment of these glass cases that my students had expected to see entering their classroom.

My one immediate asset was my 'British' voice. 'I may fall asleep during every session,' wrote another student, remembering how she felt during the first class, 'but at least I'll nod off to a pleasant sound.' But of course my peculiar accent was something of a cultural barrier. Was I being funny or was I serious? It was so difficult to tell. By the second week they had mostly decided that I was at least *trying* to be funny. It was probably British irony, that most awkward of all styles to translate. But they had been guided to their decision more by my appearance and behaviour than by what I actually said, pleasant-sounding as that might be. I was 'the man who came rushing into the classroom every week looking a little bit like a curious mixture of Rex Harrison and Jerry Lewis', another student wrote. In other words, a blatant comic.

What struck several of them during my carefully structured course was the informality sometimes reaching into chaos, and my air of helplessness in the middle of it all. 'Mr

Holroyd is very bad at looking stern.' I was surprised to read this sentence since I had been practising sternness in front of the mirror until it almost cracked. But eventually I decided that here was one student's brave stab at that sophisticated literary device, the unreliable narrator – and I annotated her essay accordingly. But I still had, they all observed, that desperate mannerism of running my fingers through my hair every few minutes ('I wonder if his grandmother ever told him that this makes one go bald'). One student drew an impression of my constantly rearranged hair underneath her description of it. 'His hair is rather wild,' she observed. 'It's amazing the way he gets it to stand up and lay flat in such a chaotic pattern. It looks like this.'

To this she added a drawing of me sitting alert and upright in a chair after one of my long research trips – a drawing which everyone happily agreed was very accurate (though perhaps this was a form of American graphic irony, it occurred to me, and with that interpretation I present it here).

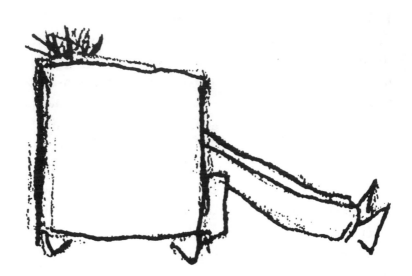

All these comments about me arose as part of (and perhaps in retaliation to) the final assignment I had set my students early on in this course. It was a literary biography and autobiography course, and as their final paper, the very essay that would carry their grades, I had asked them to write a pen portrait-in-miniature of myself. There was a gasp of genuine horror when they heard this. 'I was no longer amused,' wrote one of them, perhaps echoing Queen Victoria. Never had they heard anything so vainglorious. But then perhaps it was some trick, even a British 'joke'. I was often playing tricks on 'the poor students'. For example, among the ten or twelve books I had set for this course were a couple I disliked. Why would I choose 'a bad book' for them to read? The reason gradually became clear. I did not want them to second-guess what I thought. I did not want them trying to please me. I wanted to know what they thought themselves and to make any differing reactions to the texts the basis for our discussions. Should they deduce, therefore, that I did not want them to please me with this final paper too, the pen portrait of myself? How much hostile criticism would I accept without downgrading their papers? How much flattery could I swallow without being sick?

What I really wanted them to do was to use the library in a new way; to find out to what extent I was that person in the glass cases there; to connect the craft of reading with the craft of writing; to read between the lines of a text.

From a number of the essays they wrote, I found out that, during one of the coffee breaks, they had discussed whether or not I was homosexual. After all, I was unmarried. Also I had written a Life of Lytton Strachey and an introduction for the American edition of Quentin Crisp's *The Naked Civil Servant*. Then, too, among the autobiographies I had set them to read was a book by another homosexual author, *My Father and Myself*, by J. R. Ackerley. But there was conflicting evidence. One of my books had been warmly dedicated to a woman. A quick glance at my recently published *Augustus John* in the library revealed that he was a committed heterosexual. Perhaps it was necessary for biographers to reach beyond their instinctive interests. In the end they decided that I wasn't a homosexual. But how could they be certain? Did anyone dare ask me – and if anyone did, would I answer truthfully? Only one student pressed her enquiries further.

And that last sentence shows you what they were up against. What exactly does it mean? The American language is stronger these days than the English language. It's blunter, ruder, more muscular, demotic, direct. It is pitted, lavishly, with assholes, bombarded with one helluva lot of kicked butt, and does not boast the delicate, smooth bottom of British English. Of course English can be elegant, but its elegance is so often evasive, oblique, polite, ambiguous. It may be prettily enough served up, of course, but where in Christ's name is the big meat? Here was a cultural obstacle my students had to get round to understand my game, decode my language, discover my secrets. Why had I invited them, as it were, to play detectives, only to leave them so few clues? Though claiming to be opinionated to the very edge of libel, I seemed to have no emphatic opinions at all, certainly no emphatic political opinions (it was the time of Three Mile Island about which I appeared wonderfully inscrutable – more eager to hear my students' opinions than air my own). Where was my conviction, my 'passionate intensity'? I sounded infuriatingly cheerful, almost aggressively mild, and had more questions than conclusions – unless, that is, a conclusion may be embedded in a question (was Three Mile Island a signal from the future? I asked). The main difficulty was that I seemed so detached, too detached maybe, detached really from myself (using 'one' instead of 'I' or 'you' or 'we' sometimes when speaking, as if I were royalty, or at least not me). It was a strange and sobering performance. How could they get around it?

One evening, when the students came over for supper, we continued our discussion between drinks and I quoted a sentence written by an autobiographer who, in order to get a divorce, had been obliged to hire a French detective to report on the activities of his wife in Paris. Though her life there was a twenty-four-hour-a-day ritual of trivialities, he found the report in precise, impersonal French so unexpectedly amusing that he concluded: 'If I were a rich man, I would pay to have a French detective's report on my own movements.' My students were less amused by this aside than I was. For it reflected something of our own predicament: the distorting mirror of a different culture on the comedy of life. Besides, they said, it was taking vicariousness too far.

We sat around pouring out various odd uneven bottles, now one, then another, and I thought that this was the sort of group discussion I had missed when young, never having been at a university. Only it was focused on me because of that dreadful paper I had set. One student suggested I was wearing a self-protective mask and wondered why. Or, another student ingeniously argued, there was no mask at all, and what they were experiencing, my temperament, my voice, represented very well a country that was becoming increasingly distanced from history's active, mainstream narrative – the hectic narrative of the United States which, in the echo-chamber of our 'special relationship', we merely parodied. Or whatever. They were teasing me tremendously, getting their own back, enjoying themselves. There was much laughter as their speculations spiralled into fantasy. Or whatever indeed!

I poured myself another drink.

Or perhaps, I intervened, we should jettison that word

'or'. Our lives came to us as a series of 'ands' – one damn thing after another – and the skill of understanding them depended upon an ability to connect all sorts of views and events, not edit them so much as to make a pattern of them.

And, I went on remorselessly, if I was the man in the self-protective mask, then it would be reasonable to conclude that this mask did not resemble me in any way. Why else would I have chosen it? It must be an act of misrepresentation and as unlike me as possible.

Unless, I added, I had grown into it.

The food came to my rescue – I had by now drunk quite a lot. In this warm social atmosphere, my vague and enigmatic manner was beginning to acquire a flavour of poignancy. 'Where nothing lives, nothing can die.' Somewhere I had written or said this (written *and* said this, for, as my students pointed out, I quite often said what I had written). If I became too attached to life, would I not have more to fear from death? My apartment, they noticed, was bare – no flowers, no pictures, while in London they knew I had no domestic animals, not even a frog or stick-insect. So I was obviously a solitary. And yet, I appealed, from the centre of my crowded supper party, swaying slightly, I was gregarious. I actually liked people, some people; and also various animals. Even so, my students spied a dangerous fate in store for me, and from it they plucked a delightful solution to their problem. I had been keeping company with the dead, my biographical subjects, too long, and had set them the task of rescuing me from those glass cases in the library (even though, they reluctantly acknowledged, it was my glass-case career that had brought me over to them). There were several ways in which they set about this . . .

Next morning I had an awful hangover.

The students' final papers were written in many forms: as a diary, an obituary, a letter to a publisher; as a forward-looking science-fiction pastiche, an autobiography with myself as the significant other character, and as pure literary criticism. I had tried to bring the reading of books out of the glass case, but had also perhaps converted myself into a text.

We met, the eleven of us, Constance, David, Diane, Karen, Kate, Linda, Maureen, Miki, Terese, Thomas and me, for some three hours a week over ten to twelve weeks. And it was fun. But what they handed in, they reminded me, were merely first impressions. So what I now have are the beginnings of a self-portrait.

For the next stage, I must turn to a book first published in 1936, the year after I was born. It has on its hardback jacket a silver mirror, and it makes bold on its title page to offer 'about three million detailed individual character studies through self-analysis'. Surely this should do the trick, at least help me do it. *Meet Yourself As You Really Are** was constructed by Prince Leopold Loewenstein, a political scientist and philosopher educated at the

---

*In the United States the book was called *Analyze Yourself* and edited by Victor Rosen (1955).

University of Vienna, who later specialised in the psychology of Nazism and Fascism; and it was composed by his friend – and later mine – the novelist William Gerhardie, who had been educated in Russia and at Worcester College, Oxford. So testing a work did it prove that these co-authors, who had long been friends, split up after writing it and never spoke to each other again. It was, I sensed, a potent book.

I worked from the paperback edition, an old yellow-covered Penguin Book, No. 382, carrying advertisements which urged me to smoke Grey's Cigarettes, eat Fry's chocolates, and then go to the Pelman Institute to have my worries removed (half fees for members of His Majesty's Forces). The advice sounds bad today and the solution dubious. But I persist, tracing my psychoanalytical outlines through the complex framework of questions and instructions. I acquire a colour, yellow. Is it sunlight? Am I cowardly? Then I am given a river, the Neva which flows through St Petersburg into the Gulf of Finland (and also provides a link with the Caspian Sea). I take this as a good omen, since Gerhardie himself spent his childhood in St Petersburg. What do I find out about myself as I steer my way though these pages?

> You belong to a type of character which is composed of the most contradictory features and . . . [is] very difficult to understand. People of your type resent loneliness almost as much as the company of others . . . Quite generally it can be said that your type of character produces pronounced individualists.

But the River Neva then branches wildly, and I learn that:

> You are probably generous as far as property and money go, but we cannot give unrestricted praise to this generosity. It is not the expression of a happy and well-balanced disposition. You resemble, though it might seem somewhat strange to you, your very opposite type – the avaricious . . . There is something destructive in this exaggerated tendency to give.

Reading this, I am reminded of an episode from the 1970s which reveals what it was like to be on the receiving end of my help. I had been asked to write the prefaces for a reissue of William Gerhardie's works, but soon found that he considered my praise of his books insufficiently unqualified. My avariciousness was evidently showing through my generosity and it threatened, he believed, to destroy his posthumous reputation, or at least to impair it. In exasperation, he berated me for being 'a *smilingly* impenitent, pig-headed, bloody-minded, bigoted, intolerant, unyielding, unelastic, *hard*, inflexible, opinionated, fanatical, obsessed, pedantic, rook-ribbed, *unmoved*, persistent, incurable, irrepressible, intractable, impersuadable, cross-grained ruffian – no offence implied'. And none taken. Eventually I was to solve the problem by reading my prefaces to him over the telephone instead of sending them by post, raising my voice through a magnificent crescendo as I bellowed out passages of unrestricted praise, then dropping to a modest whisper when delivering the lesser sentences.

This scheme of orchestration, which worked well, should probably earn me several extra epithets from the thesaurus: cunning, tricky, artful, prankish, *unblushing*, foxy, scheming, Machiavellian, *double-tongued*, unstraightforward, devious, slippery, shameless, fly . . .

A self-portrait, I see, is beginning to emerge. I go back to the book to find out if I have any more luck. The River Neva takes me in my yellow submarine to the next landing stage.

> You are not the type of person whose company is sought after by others, except by those you know really well. But how does one get to know you really well? You do not make it too easy. You do not talk readily about your inner struggles and the problems that beset your mind. You are rather like a sick person who does not want others to know he is ill.

I seem to remember that when I last played this game twenty or thirty years ago, I came out rather better than this. My character is deteriorating. How far can this go?

> You are at war with yourself for being at peace with the world. You find it is more than life is worth to fight the world, and you are far too frank to humbug yourself . . . your capacity for suffering is out of all proportion to the use you can make of it.

I throw the book across the room. The trouble has been

that I can answer many of the guiding questions with equal accuracy one way or another. But when I attempt to follow other tributaries of my river, I fare no better. No wonder the book was never a bestseller. It does not flatter its readers.

But the process of stitching together these paragraphs to fit myself brings to mind another refitting exercise. This took place in the 1990s at the University of Ulster at Coleraine. Having misread my invitation, I arrived without a dinner jacket. Since my name was to be mentioned in a speech during the dinner, all eyes would be turned on me, the only guest inadequately clothed. This could not be. Alerted to the crisis, the departments of the university came collectively to my rescue. From the Faculty of Engineers arrived a splendid tuxedo; from 'Life and Health', a fine shirt; from 'Informatics' some dazzling cufflinks; and from the Social Sciences a terrific bow tie. But the wonder of it all was that everything fitted me perfectly. As I went through into dinner, I looked smarter, faster, more tailor-made for success than I could possibly have done in my own best clothes. My students at Penn State, and those non-speaking authors of *Meet Yourself*, would not have recognised me.

'It's over. All over. Nearly over.' But hold on. To complete this assisted self-portrait I need an authentic end. How to convey the sense of an ending when it is 'not the end'? Not quite. I call on absence and the blank page to see me out. 'What Might Have Been' is a poem I have kept since it was sent to me many years ago.

Mosaic

Now that you've really gone
And not forever bobbing
Just out of reach

Now that not streets and weeks
But months and an ocean
Lie between us

Now that I look
Into a calm grey distance
And see (as you have always done)

What might have been
As not a blue-print or a sketch
But a finished work

That couldn't be improved upon –
Each line we've added since
A weakening – I am beginning

To understand at last
What you meant when you said
'I am best at absence.'

5

Philippa

HER STORY

... I cannot see the flowers so sweet
I cannot smell and I cannot weep
And I cannot wake and I cannot sleep.
For I who laughed and loved am dead,
And laid out on my cold white bed,
With my jaw tied up lest it give offence
And my eyelids closed with a couple of pence ...
It seems a senseless thing to die!

Frank Harris

But Margaret Forster's letter has not yet reached its end. 'I wondered a lot about your beautiful mother, and the effect her beauty had on you as a young man, and on your girl friends,' she persisted. 'You describe how proud you were of her appearance when you were at school, but I wondered about later, when you were, say, 25 or so, and she was an incredibly young looking 43, so exquisitely dressed & lovely – what kind of ideas did it give you about women in general, & how did it influence your love life?'

I do not know the answers to these questions, and feel a great resistance to answering them. But other readers, too, have chided me. So I shall try to fill one more gap in my story.

When I was twenty-five or so, I was having my first sexual experiences with prostitutes. This was not because I preferred sex with strangers, or wanted to feel superior to women, or needed to separate sex from friendship and love, but because it was the only sexual experience straightforwardly available to me. My mother and father, going their separate ways, and so many ways, had not helped to integrate me into any community. Though I still saw one or two schoolfriends, I was a floating, solitary figure, incapacitated by all the familiar ineptitudes of youth – shyness, self-consciousness, lack of confidence – that I retained far too long. Yet I was extremely susceptible to women – and many women appeared beautiful to me. Having no sisters, and confined so long within the male worlds of boarding schools and National Service, I had no habit of companionship with women, though in later life I was to find their companionship easier and generally more rewarding than that of men.

I walked all over London in those days and nights – especially the nights. I would walk for hours, anywhere, everywhere, tiring myself out so that I could eventually sleep. Sometimes I would lose myself in strange streets, striding along until I found myself back on course, thinking about all sorts of possibilities – people, usually, and paragraphs. I looked at the places I passed in all weathers, but more intently at the people, and flattered myself that I was like Dickens in his young days (perhaps I was so far as the mileage went).

In the 1950s many streets in London were lined, under the lights, with prostitutes. I would set off for my long exhausting walks, and occasionally, if I had amassed three pounds (a considerable sum), I would go with one of them.

In anticipation, I felt a trembling excitement, as if I were entering the first stages of a romantic adventure, but afterwards no French novel was to develop round me and I remained solitary. Nevertheless, I did not regret spending my money in this way. It seemed completely natural and necessary – all the more so since sex before marriage for girls was still rare in those days.

Not having read Bernard Shaw, I did not equate the crowds of prostitutes in those lurid pools of light with Britain's post-war poverty, though I did recognise in it a legacy from Victorian London. When, in 1959, R. A. Butler's Street Offences Act virtually cleared prostitutes from the streets, a new age was launched combining official puritanism with the beginnings of 'free love' – and distancing the language and legislation of Westminster further from actual life, street life. The streets themselves were eventually to be populated by beggars and vagrants (unknown before the 1970s) who pitched their mattresses under bridges, in doorways and anywhere else made available in the expanding ground between rich and poor.

In *Basil Street Blues* I described how I later met and fell into bed with my first girlfriend, Jennifer, a ballet dancer from the north, and I quoted her shrewd and vivid comments on my mother and father. After several years together, she gave me an ultimatum: either we married or she left. Otherwise there was no future. But I was beginning to enjoy living in the present. I had no desire to marry, probably as a result of my parents' many unsuccessful marriages and the difficulties these had provided. So we parted, Jennifer and myself, with immense sadness on both sides. I remember watching her walk away to the end of the street and turn the corner out of my life, not knowing what would happen next. She did not look back.

By then, entering my thirties, I suddenly found myself becoming quite popular with women, some women, and had several affaires. I was not stubbornly 'faithful' to anyone, nor (despite the pain of jealousy) did I question anyone's faithfulness to me. These were games of love we were all playing in the 1960s, serious, delightful, with moments of anguish, beauty and farce. As for myself, it was as if I were copying my parents' promiscuous emotional lives unburdened by the complications and formalities of marriage and divorce. Though I said and did many silly things, and was sometimes insensitive through incomprehension, I look back on this time as being vital and necessary. One of the advantages of low self-esteem and a slow start is that many happenings which others seem to take for granted – driving a car, publishing a book, having a love affair – strike you as miraculous. Certainly for me the late 1960s still has the distant glow of a miracle.

Everything changed dramatically towards the end of that decade, when I became involved with an extraordinary girl called Philippa Pullar. I met her at a dinner party given by the editor who was publishing my *Lytton Strachey* (she was a friend of his wife). A young American writer, Stanley Olson, was to describe Philippa two or three years later as 'the sexiest middle-aged – 30 – woman I've ever seen. Every word is like a mini-orgasm – she's splendid.' Certainly I thought her splendid that evening. The atmosphere around her seemed to reverberate with fantasy, infinitely hopeful yet charged with alarm, even danger – especially danger. Nevertheless, here was someone who, even on the very worst of days, lived under a brilliant sun. Her luminous presence brightened everything near her. She had an oval face, long, blonde hair to her shoulders, piercing blue eyes and a small straight nose – but the truly remarkable feature was her voice. It was highly theatrical, mannered and melodramatic, also rather camp, full of exaggerated emphasis, unlike any voice I had heard. She used it to great comic effect, but initially, like many people, I felt disconcerted, wondering whether it was an affectation put on for dinner parties. Only when I got to know her better did I come to realise what perfect orchestration this voice gave to the expression of seething rebelliousness within her. She took the accents of smart society and sent them up rotten. She made conventional manners sound farcical, speaking with an exhilaration that testified to the urgency of her need – a need to escape the suffocating conformity in which she had been brought up. Her spectacular personality was like some incandescent shell that concealed and protected an acute sensitivity.

Her father had been 'a creature of convention' and 'a victim of respectability', who lived in scowling silent horror of Jews and gypsies, socialists, homosexuals and all other so-called hooligans. Having served in one world war, he passed the next, while Philippa was growing up, somewhere in the West Country carrying out duties 'suitable to his rank of major'. Philippa herself was moved from house to house avoiding the bombs and scuttling into shelters with her mother, who was of a highly nervous disposition. 'I was a delicate child and a constant worry to my mother,' she remembered. She was also, from the very first, a surprise, her mother having been told that she could never have children – and then conceiving her daughter when in her forties.

Philippa did not know that her highly conventional mother was the illegitimate daughter of a free-thinking woman who had left her husband and eloped with the son of a Scottish nobleman. Both died in the flu pandemic of 1920, leaving their only child (Philippa's mother) to be brought up by an elderly governess. It was no wonder then that she longed for Philippa, her only daughter, to be respectable and safe, or that she unconsciously passed on to her a vibrant sense of insecurity. In the mother this took the form of an acute anxiety over the uncertainties of daily life; with Philippa it eventually focused on death.

Her childhood friend, Clare Michell, remembers how, from her earliest years, Philippa longed to escape the protective embrace of her mother, and how wild she would sometimes be when she got away. On a school holiday in Austria, the train having broken down in a deep snowdrift near Innsbruck, Philippa climbed through a gap at the top of the compartment window, ran along the snowbank outside the train, and was later seen being chased back along the top of the carriages by amorous waiters. 'We were all very impressed by her daring,' recalls Clare. Another time Clare remembers how scandalised people were to see her whizzing along on a bicycle beside a French canal pursued by (or was it pursuing?) a wild boar. 'One forgets how staid people were in the 1950s.'

Philippa stood out from her schoolfriends, not being dependent on their company. 'She wanted to run things rather than join them,' Clare Michell wrote, 'and didn't like being upstaged.' Some of these schoolfriends believed she would become a famous actress, like 'the terrific Kemble'. Henry James's description of the 'lavishly décolletée' Fanny Kemble also gives a good and lasting impression of Philippa in her many roles: 'joking, punning, botanising, encouraging the lowly and abusing the proud, making stupidity gape . . . and startling infallibly all primness and propriety'. The great nineteenth-century actress, James adds, 'assisted at the social comedy of her age' with the originality and gaiety of her 'admirable nonsense': and so, in her fashion, did Philippa.

But of course the stage was unacceptable to her parents. Philippa's father wanted her to behave well; her mother wanted her to dress well: and in their opinions she positively did neither. From being a delicate child she grew into a riotous tomboy who was expelled from her first boarding school at the age of thirteen for writing a sexually explicit work of fantasy. It took the form of a correspondence between herself, in the role of a dashing young lover, and her best friend as the beloved, beginning innocently and then blossoming into imagined consummation ('It was lovely to feel a bit of me inside you' etc.). From her next school (which specialised in deportment and embroidery in a house that had belonged to the anti-suffrage novelist Mrs Humphry Ward) she was also expelled following what she called 'a run of bad luck' which began when her pony Chocolate, famous for his extravagant co-ordination of bucking and farting, chased the riding mistress up a tree.

Her parents then decided that she must 'do the Season', find a suitable husband, and settle down. Quickly. Her mother would see to her clothes, dressing her up like a pink doll, while her father, though seldom breaking his silence, would somehow convey the modest behaviour that was required of her. Later on, Philippa was to write a brief history of the London Season, the last chapter of which featured her own debutante exploits while 'coming out' during Coronation Year. She was taught how to curtsey by Madame Vacani, how to put on make-up properly by Hermione Gingold, and how to dance correctly to Tommy Kinsman's band ('you leant slightly backwards, shoulders not moving, the right arm stretched down towards the floor, and if one were in love – or fast – the fingers were linked together').

To her parents' relief Philippa became engaged to Robin, a young man with a beautiful house in Carmarthenshire. 'I was as much in love with the place as the man himself,' she later admitted. His sudden death before their marriage shocked her profoundly. 'Never before had I seen serious illness: the fear, the blood transfusion tubes, the struggling for breath, the vomiting,' she wrote. 'My world had shattered . . . I was distraught.'

Mourning her own pain, she took up and then gave up a succession of jobs over the next three years – as a waitress in Chelsea, a cook in Soho, an air hostess. She became well known for her wild parties and for the impressive quantities of alcohol she drank. In desperation, her parents relaunched her into the marriage market of the London Season. Though social life was beginning to change radically in Britain, the structure of the Season still stood intact (though 1958 was the last year that debutantes were individually presented to the Queen). 'Isn't it sad,' one of the mothers remarked, looking over the banisters in Grosvenor House at the lines of daughters rehearsing their ridiculous 'curtseying to the cake' for Queen Charlotte's Ball. 'They are *en route* to the kitchen sink.'

Philippa (whose maiden name was King) married Robert Pullar because by this time all her friends were married. He had been proposing to her for a long time, enticed, so she believed, by her unavailability – she had been adamant, following Robin's death, that she would never marry. As soon as she accepted him, she knew it was a mistake. At night she was tormented by awful dreams; by day she took herself in hand and carried on with the marriage arrangements.

They went to live in Devon where, having lost his capital in a failed agricultural equipment company, her husband took to raising battery hens, at which he also failed – but which gave rise to Philippa's passionate hatred of factory farming and a crusading kindness on behalf of all animals. She felt imprisoned by this marriage, a prey to Satanic hallucinations, on the very edge of madness. Everyone told her she would feel better once she had children. She had two sons, and felt worse. She accepted responsibility for her children, but was not a good mother, resenting the implication that women who were not natural mothers must be inferior women. 'I would wonder how it was possible to be so miserable,' she later wrote. 'This was hell, that at least I knew.'

In the mid-1960s the two of them left Devon and separated, he going to work in London, she buying a house in Deal (which had once been owned by the judge who convicted Oscar Wilde). It was during this period that I met her at dinner. She wrote down her telephone number that evening on a book of matches and handed it to me. A few days later I rang her and went down to Deal for a weekend. On the Saturday night we slept together in her bed. I remember the softness of her skin, her musky smell and how young she suddenly looked, would always suddenly look, with her head on the pillow. By Sunday, we decided that we wanted to go on seeing each other. There is 'a marvellous cosiness about sex', Philippa later wrote; 'there in the room with the fire blazing you could make someone secure, if only for a brief moment, for it seemed to me that many men were haunted by sadness: they yearned for contact, communication – some even longed for love. And for a brief interlude sex gave them release from their isolation.'

In the Prologue to her book *The Shortest Journey* (1981), Philippa was to give me the name Horace (after Horace Walpole). I was, she wrote, 'the perfect antidote to my husband: gentle, sensitive and intelligent: an author working on a long biography of an eminent man of letters.

He educated me, introduced me to music, books and

ideas . . . gradually and creakingly, my brain began to function . . . When Horace and I were together it was as though an electrical spark flew between us, igniting some force that was both invigorating and cleaving. We were both of us stimulated, full of verve, and we *laughed*. I calmed down considerably . . .

Horace altered my way of thinking. Horace altered my attitude of mind. Certainly I did not want to marry, but I did want to be with Horace.

Philippa was to describe me as her 'second teacher', her first teacher being Chocolate, the exuberant pony which had swerved and bolted with her across the English countryside, taking her everywhere and opening up in her a new feeling for the land: 'the crushed turf of the downs redolent with wild thyme; damp earth mixed with bluebells; gorse; hay; the tarred string of hay nets; saddle soap and the warm sweaty breath of Chocolate himself. Celandines shone in the spring, the ground drummed in winter with white frost.'

What Chocolate had taught Philippa, she taught me. Life grew more tangible and vivid. I began to use my eyes, to see the visible world around me with greater subtlety, enjoyment and understanding. It was as if a veil had been removed. I spent many days and nights at Deal, which I came to see through Philippa's eyes. Her eighteenth-century house faced both west and east. On the west side stood a conservatory, full of the scent of flowers, and a walled garden, with its central quince tree, framed by the tiled roofs of houses nearby. In summer, the vine hung with muscat grapes. Jasmine, tobacco and datura, whose white bells bent over the pond, filled the air with a heavy fragrance. On the east side was the sea over which, at low tides, you could make out the masts of ships that had been wrecked on the Goodwin Sands.

Walking along the cliffs at evening, we appeared to float in the dusk, looking down on the childlike boats below. On late still afternoons, a cricket would sometimes sing in the garden, as if we were by the Mediterranean. This garden attracted all sorts of butterflies – I had not seen so many since I was a boy – tortoiseshells, chalk blues and purple emperors that wandered around the lavender, fennel and savory. Whenever possible we ate in the garden and would watch the moon rise from the sea like some dull, red ball growing gradually into a huge corn-coloured orb that appeared to be attached to us by triangular paths of light along the surface of the water.

But magical as these summers were, it was the autumn, with strange evening mists, the dartings of the swifts and swallows through the air, the mournful serenade of foghorns sounding along the curve of the beach and mixing with the rhythmic chanting of the pigeons, the whistling of the starlings, that held a more poignant beauty. I had never experienced before anything of such lingering intensity. It was as if I had suddenly woken up to all that was around me, as if everything was coming for the first time into focus.

But then there were the winters. As the nights drew in, we fixed storm windows on the front of the house against the icy wind and the rain beating in, sometimes ferociously, from the

Straits of Dover. It accelerated along the narrow tunnels of the streets, making Deal a winter fortress under siege. From November to February, no sun reached the garden which lay in perpetual shadow, its trees angrily swaying, like the landscape of a dark underworld.

Philippa's moods matched the seasons, and there were times when she would feel miserably incarcerated at Deal, with her two sons, several cats and a parrot as her gaolers. To remedy this I suggested that we rent an inexpensive flat in London, so that to some extent she could escape this horror of imprisonment.

We found a rather seedy maisonette on the top two floors of a house in West Kensington. It was infested with mice which soon made friends with the free-range, multiplying guinea pigs which Philippa had unaccountably brought back one night from a party. 'Meet Philippa, meet her animals,' wrote Mike Foss who visited us there.

When her key was in the lock, a rustling of light squeals began beyond the door. The guinea pigs were welcoming her home . . .

I think she liked them because they were droll and fat and happy, and that was a good state for any animal. There were also some cats, one with three legs . . . The three-legged one got no special favours but shared the rewards of residence, and the fleas, impartially. Philippa was scornful of mollycoddlying, for cats or humans. Three legs were plenty for a cat. A determination to enjoy life was what counted. The accidental loss of a leg was merely an incident, a test of character. The cat seemed to know this. It didn't fret.

Mike Foss, then an aspiring writer who contributed reviews to *Tribune*, first met Philippa in a pub. 'There was something nautical in her confident gait,' he remembers noticing as she cleaved her way through the press of noisy male drinkers.

Planting herself firmly between us, she started immediately, as if she had known me for years, to tell me an improbable tale that verged on disaster but was resolved into a condition of farce and puzzlement. At the same time she reached an absent-minded hand into the sandwich cabinet, extracted a scotch egg, and began to eat it with much criticism of its texture and taste, though the egg was unordered and unpaid for. 'If they put these things on the bar,' she said brusquely, 'what can they expect?' I saw, for the first of many times, a look of amused consternation on Michael's face.

On the ground floor of our London flat was Mrs del Rio, a harmless widow who wandered in all weathers very slowly round her tiny garden pursued by an elderly cat. Above her, and below us, lived the formidable Mrs Harvey, an aggressive old lady who was rumoured to write poetry and to have been imprisoned in China. She was 'at war with herself and with everyone else in the world', wrote Philippa, who pictured her as a twentieth-century London witch.

She wore a strange brown habit, bubbled evil-smelling concoctions in her kitchen and piped abuse ... in a terrible quavering wail. She planted wooden cats' heads in her window-boxes and watered them, their drips combining with those from the lavatory brush suspended from the window-sill ... No one was unaffected by Mrs Harvey's delusions, which were quickened alarmingly by the full moon – it was rather like living in a sea resort and being governed by the tides.

Mrs Harvey suspected Philippa and me of being spies. Having fixed up an emergency notice on the front door reading 'PRIVAT LETTER CAGE' (an 'E' having gone missing in the heat of her passion), she would mail our letters back to the Post Office marked 'NOT Known Here'. This was particularly exasperating for me as I vainly waited for letters of congratulation on my recently published *Lytton Strachey*. Once, when we invited a venerable member of the Bloomsbury Group to lunch and were saying our polite goodbyes in the street below, Mrs Harvey suddenly loomed over us on her balcony, waving her lavatory brush. 'Vile woman!' she screeched, gaining an immediate audience of builders from the scaffolding opposite, and schoolchildren making their way back home. 'Your morals match your vermin, madam!' Another day, I invited my father to lunch so that he could meet Philippa. Mrs Harvey, who had by then decided that we were running a betting shop to conceal our spying activities, shot out of her door and tried to arrest him on the staircase, roaring out as she grappled with him: 'Pretending to place *another* bet, are you?'

My father was profoundly bewildered by Philippa and everything that went on around her. He could never quite get his balance in her company. If he had a slightly risqué anecdote from the Twenties or Thirties up his sleeve, she would have a more outrageous contemporary tale to cap it – and it came from all over her person, never just her sleeve. I remember her telling the story of a party she had gone to with some Russians. Considering the quantities of vodka they had drunk, it was just as well that her car was not working that evening. She caught the last bus back and ended the night in bed with the conductor (it was a number 14 bus, she recalled). Turning to my father, sitting there in his suit, she exclaimed: 'Really, my dear, it's easier these days to get *oneself* serviced than one's car!' My father, who usually enjoyed talking about cars, was speechless. He tried to gain the initiative. When he came down to Deal, he ordered some oysters and, while giving us a rather complicated tutorial on how best to open them, suddenly fainted, collapsing with a bang on to the floor. Somehow he could not assert himself. A committed dog-lover, he was never quite at ease among the flocks of guinea pigs and rabbits, the cats and parrot. How could he take a rabbit for a walk? It was frankly impossible. Back in the safety of his flat in Surrey, alone with his dog, he would chuckle with amusement, remembering some of Philippa's eccentricities. But really, he thought, she was a high explosive. Using his special low voice, speaking with paternal gravity, clearing his throat a good deal, he would remind me that she was still married with two sons, and then, his voice descending still further until I could hardly pick up what he was saying, he would warn me against marriage after her divorce came through. He had made this sort of mistake himself. 'So I know what I'm talking about, Michael,' he would say – and then grow suddenly silent as if realising that, had he not made this mistake with my mother, I would not be sitting opposite him.

My mother was also puzzled by Philippa, who struck her as being so extravagantly English that, when they met, she herself became excessively Swedish. I felt as if I were their interpreter. There was a foreignness between them – and a wry understanding. Their early years must have been marked by a good many similarities, including a determination to make up for the remoteness of their parents with a hectic social and sexual life. But Philippa was already finding sources of happiness other than the love of men: in her plants and animals, later in her writing, and finally in the comforts of esoteric religion. My mother, on the other hand, though with lessening conviction, went on playing the same game, as if the clock had never moved on and she had not grown older.

When, aged around sixty and no longer in receipt of a 'pension' from her Viennese ex-lover Egon, my mother began to find life in London financially impossible, Philippa offered her free use of the maisonette that was attached to her house in Deal and which she sometimes rented out. But my mother refused. She still thought of London as offering everything that was attractive and exciting in life, whereas Philippa was beginning to feel that, as she wrote in *Gilded Butterflies* (1978): 'London has always had a disastrous effect on people.'

London certainly seemed to be having a disastrous effect on us, as if Mrs Harvey was aiming dreadful spells at us through the ceiling, spells that rose with the malodorous fumes of her cooking. Philippa grew seriously ill. One of the causes was her writing. She needed to make some money and it was obviously more practical for her to work at home, as I was doing. She had decided to write a book that would enable her to vent her hostility to intensive farming, and to attack the money motive that seemed to be growing up everywhere around her. It was to be a most ambitious work – a compendium of all she most hated in a world that, she was discovering, concealed so much cruelty under its polite veneer. The main text of this book was the diary of misery she had kept while living with her husband in Devon. She opened it and read once more the excruciating descriptions of the chickens they had kept in tiny cages, some of them blind, all with their bodies raw from constant friction against iron bars, and with their beaks electrically amputated (a harrowing process, 'ghastly with gasps, sizzling and blood'). She heard again what seemed to her their screams of distress from those awful prisons at the end of the garden. She remembered having to drive them in their crates to be slaughtered – 'hauled out and hooked upside down on a conveyor belt and, flapping what was left of their poor wings, they rotated to their death'. At night she dreamt of their dead bodies, limp and dangling, their eyes white, their throats cut – she could hear the knife ripping into the flesh and would start awake screaming. She felt she *was* those chickens, painfully confined, destined for awful death. Her nightmares began to invade the day. She had hallucinations, and saw Satan sitting at a table in the kitchen, grinning at her. The horror and misery of ten years before returned. She hated herself, her malevolent nervous system, and she hated a world that was bursting with such pain. She did not want to belong to such a place. Her moods lurched and swerved violently, unaccountably – she swallowed purple hearts, anti-depressants, sleeping pills, all mixed with alcohol. It was impossible to tell what effect they were having. I believe she would have come through had her book been accepted. It contained many strong passages, but was uncoordinated, in places incoherent. A good editor might have rescued it, made it acceptable, harnessed its power and originality. But this would have taken time and skill. I could not do it – it was *her* book – and though I could provide bits and pieces of help, I knew I must not trespass. It was a wonder how, in such exhausting circumstances, she had managed to complete it. Like an SOS she sent it out, but no one answered. She felt rejected.

One morning after breakfast, while we were in the kitchen, she casually mentioned that, having watched the chairs and table dancing grotesquely round the room, she had swallowed several handfuls of sleeping tablets. She had had enough. Though she sometimes had delusions, she never told lies. As soon as I felt certain this was not a fantasy, I went to the telephone, dialled 999, and summoned an ambulance. I tried to keep her upright and walking till I heard the siren of the ambulance approaching. The paramedics fought their way up past the yelling Mrs Harvey and took Philippa to the hospital where she had her stomach pumped. Had we been an hour later, I was told, she would probably have died.

And here, as Philippa recovers in hospital, I must pause to consider the implication of what happened. For this was not to be the only suicide attempt by someone I loved. There would be one other that, unintentionally, ended in tragedy. What can I deduce from this? I believe I have sometimes been attracted to women who, in lay terms, may be described as manic-depressive. The manic aspect of their personality eclipses my mother's beauty, and I am mesmerised – to the extent of not comprehending, not wishing to comprehend, the dark hidden side of their personalities to which my intelligence should alert me. I am frightened of depression, nonplussed, made inert. But I have a personality that may, at first sight, attract the manic-depressive. For I am like a tightrope-walker who has had to find a perilous route between the extravagances of my mother's and my father's separate lives. So I appear, on my tightrope, to be miraculously balanced – and this feat of balance has its own appeal for those in danger of plunging, one way or another, into extremes. Also, I know that some women came to feel that I was not sufficiently taken care of by my parents. So, with my two birthdays, I am again two people: the boy whose lack of love can be made good; and the father-figure, with his elevated balance and even-handedness, a figure of tall authority. Yet this authority has its limits and the tightrope its distance.

There is another question that occurs to me and that I must try to answer. Do I have an unconscious wish to punish my mother, who often left me while I was growing up? And have I turned the need for revenge on to other women? The fact that I am completely unconscious of such a motive and do not pick it up even as a faint echo, does not of course invalidate the possibility of an unconscious motive. But the devastation I have felt, the long period of grief, is the evidence I would bring forward to refute this suggestion. In short: I do not believe it to be true.

What I did learn from Philippa's illness was the irrelevance of my good sense, the uselessness of my logic and reasonableness. She was beyond reason. But she also appeared to be beyond the help of her doctors – it was they who had given her those almost fatal pills. She also went to a psychoanalyst but was, she confessed, unable to help him.

One doctor informed her that she was suffering from serious hormonal imbalance aggravated by the contraceptive pills she was taking. In the ensuing muddle of dates and other pills, various sheaths and some medieval-looking devices, Philippa became pregnant. There was no question of her having another child – she was far too unstable. At first, with my aid, she experimented with several ancient recipes for inducing a miscarriage – drinking gin in hot baths and brewing up pungent herbal concoctions laced with vinegar that mingled in the air with Mrs Harvey's venomous boiled cabbages. When all this failed she consulted her doctor. But

127

getting an abortion was not then easy. The weeks ticked on as she went off to be examined by doctors and psychiatrists. She told them about her attempted suicide, described the Satanic hallucinations, her chronic depression, and the fears she had of going insane – all encircling dangers for a baby. It was a matter, as I saw it, of making these doctors more frightened of the consequences of not allowing her to have an abortion than of any criticism arising from the charge of unnecessarily taking a life. Eventually, after some four months, they consented and I drove her to the hospital.

Did I mind not having a child? Not at all. My single thought then was for Philippa's health (on which my own depended). Did I mind later? Do I mind now? The answer is the same. It has never worried me, and I have hardly thought of it until now. Why, then, don't I mind? It has, I believe, something to do with my own childhood and family rather than the fear of seeing more love go to the child than to myself or of my own childish side being eclipsed by a genuine child. I got on quite well, I think, I hope, with Philippa's sons, though I was careful to see that I never came near to replacing their father. Indeed there was no question of that. They spent half their holidays with their father, and were soon going to boarding schools, so I saw little enough of them both. The elder son, sensible, down to earth, began to feel, I thought, that his mother was a bit mad. Sebastian, the younger son, sometimes pretended to be a guinea pig or cat in order to get more loving attention from her. She treated them both in as carefree a way as possible. No doubt they were up to something, something inadvisable, but it was not her concern; no doubt they had their own plans and would not welcome her interference. Had Philippa wanted another child, I would have felt nervous, but would not have objected. And then I would be able to answer these questions with greater validity.

Philippa herself, I thought, took the abortion very matter-of-factly. But when I went to collect her, hurrying her along somewhat because the car outside was parked on double yellow lines, I saw for a moment tears in her eyes. I have not forgotten that.

We had both been profoundly shocked, and recognised the need to review and reorganise our lives together. My plan of living in two places so as to alleviate Philippa's fear of being trapped, though superficially appealing, had not worked well, even after I learnt to drive the car – a stubborn, bad-tempered, snorting old monster that had once been a proud and stately Austin. Much of our time seemed held in traffic jams along the M2, then in the process of being constructed, the car overflowing with bowls of soup, flowers, fruit, typewriters, miscellaneous papers, cats, guinea pigs and grumbling children. Instead of providing freedom, our dual town-and-country life grew into a whirlwind of anxiety, incompetence, exhaustion and irritability. My instinct was to simplify life, Philippa's instinct was to enrich it. Each was a good corrective to the other, complementary in good times but in bad times mutually destructive. How could we make the bad times good?

Our solution was: *rus in urbe*. Philippa sold the beautiful house in Deal, we gave up what we now thought of as our

haunted maisonette in West Kensington, and bought a
Victorian house on the frontiers of Putney and Barnes. *Urbe*
was all round us: in the trains that clattered and rumbled past
the end of the garden; and the aeroplanes that flew just above
us on the flightpath to Heathrow; and also in new tower
blocks of flats that intermittently blocked out the sun in
winter. But the house stood in an unadopted private road on
the frontiers of the country, next to an open common where
cricket was played in summer, fairs and circuses camped in
the winter.

And there was space, both in the house and especially in
the garden with its mulberry tree at the centre up which
Philippa trained white roses. Like the quince tree at Deal, this
mulberry tree, with its red and white blooms, gave a strange,
fairytale atmosphere to the garden, ever-changing and
extraordinary, where you could easily lose yourself.
Philippa grew honeysuckle and clematis up the walls (and
over some of the windows), made the rectangular shape of
the ground appear wonderfully asymmetrical, full of
surprises, with curving paths leading to a naked wooden
statue, some trickling water, a kitchen garden, much of all
this concealed by a rich texture of plants and shrubs. She
designed a conservatory, dug a pond in it, and then filled it
with enormous fish that were so fiercely tame they appeared,
as we sat there in the evenings, to be trying to come out and
settle on our laps. Certainly the fish alarmed the cats. Indoors
and out-of-doors, jumping in and out through the open
windows, there was room for all the animals – to which she
added various frogs and a spectacular black cockerel to

which, as the writer Andrew Barrow* remembers, she sometimes flung slices of continental cheese.

The house became a wonderful stage for Philippa's dramatic talents. There were heavy, theatrical curtains fitted by an Amazonian young woman whose unusual window-boxes confronted Scotland Yard – years later, after her marriage had been annulled, she became Princess Michael of Kent. These curtains, pinned back but apt to shoot sideways unprovoked, suited Philippa's personality. Her friend, the psychotherapist Andrew McCall, thought of her as a natural actress – how else was one to reconcile the many contradictions of her personality? At one time she would act poor, another time wealthy; she could be fiercely chaste and then again extraordinarily promiscuous. When Andrew observed that none of the bedside lamps in the house worked, she replied that it would be 'inauspicious' to sleep with the electrician – evidently the notion of paying him had not occurred to her, for at that phase of the moon she was poor and chaste. This problem was eventually solved by Eduardo Sant'Anna whom she commissioned to install electrical wiring in the lodger's room and who 'soon afterwards became the lodger myself. We had an agreement where, instead of paying the full rent, I would do the house

---

*Andrew Barrow courageously invited Philippa and Germaine Greer to a celebratory dinner for Quentin Crisp (whose *The Naked Civil Servant* was being shown on television). They 'brought out the worst in each other', Crisp decided after a vociferous argument broke out between them, completely upstaging him and silencing their host.

131

cleaning for her.' As a foreigner, he instinctively venerated her English eccentricity. 'She never failed to amaze me even when I was supposed to take her seriously,' he writes to me. 'Instead of adding salt and pepper to the dishes she created, she sometimes put in an ingredient like onion or cinnamon to bring the whole thing alive, and it did. Even the weeds in her garden were treated as delicacies.'

She liked shopping in the North End Road market, but would annoy the stallholders by picking up, and making off with, fruit and vegetables that had accidentally fallen from their barrows into the gutter. For clothes she shopped largely at jumble sales, but from time to time would take herself off to some smart shop in the West End. There was no telling how she would make her entry at a party.

We lived on the very edge of chaos. 'It was not straightforward pandemonium,' Stanley Olson observed. In the kitchen, there were no handles on the taps, so we used pliers. Every electrical gadget had developed a life of its own and needed to be coaxed, spoken to gently, as if it were an extra animal. All this was oddly mixed with various family heirlooms, such as the smart, silver dinner service she inherited from her parents. She kept the silver and brass surfaces within the house highly polished, so that their sparkle appeared to light up dark areas of the rooms. These rooms were often vastly untidy, but full of idiosyncratic beauty. She had a distinctive style – an eye for unusual objects, strong colours and striking juxtapositions – and a liking for comfort that seemed oriental in its indulgence. We had huge wood fires made of logs, trees, pieces of furniture, odd fencing, all brought back from walks and fed to the lively flames which, like a many-tongued hydra, reached out and sought to devour the room. Great urns containing mixtures of flowers appeared to give out light, piles of miscellaneous books rose from the floor like stalagmites; esoteric carpets, that had suddenly taken Philippa's fancy, seemed as if they might magically ascend. On the walls, covered with green, yellow or even purple paint or sometimes a blue book linen she had discovered in France, hung large paintings of birds and unicorns and, in her bathroom, hung slightly askew, an interesting nude of herself. This bathroom was next to her study and had a deep, old-fashioned tub grandly raised on a platform at its centre, with an easy chair beside it. While the bath was running, a friend, some historian or painter (Mike Foss, maybe, or Stella Wilkinson) might occupy the chair for a continuing chat while Philippa, in a dressing-gown, tested the water and made her preparations.

I had then begun writing my Life of Augustus John, and it seemed to me that Philippa possessed a similar instinct for beauty as that of the legendary Dorelia John. By opening my eyes to the visible world, she enabled me to write of Dorelia's houses with their mixed smells of lavender and pomanders, wood and tobacco smoke, their haphazard piles of apples and nuts, soft lead tubes of paint, old saddles, arrangements of flowers taken from her flourishing gardens full of beehives, vegetables and caravan children, at Alderney Manor and Fryern Court. I could also write of the solitary landscapes in Wales and France that had quickened Augustus's imagination.

Philippa herself was now working on a new book. The idea for it had come to her as the result of a conversation we had over supper in Deal with the novelist Simon Raven. He had been banished from London by his publisher Anthony Blond, and lived in lodging houses at Deal – an outwardly dull, unchattering, regimented life designed to support his writing. But there was nothing dull about his conversation. Like Monsieur Jourdain, he spoke prose – a charming mixture of politeness and indecency, full of gossip, wit, and allusions to his love of cricket and classical literature. He was a big man, red-faced, mild-mannered with a volcanic soldier's laugh and the aesthete's delicacy when referring to indelicate matters (which he often did). His reputation, lit up by rumours of gambling and ambiguous sexual adventures, was lurid, but he maintained a respectable, semi-military exterior and was a martyr to his timepiece. As an outsider with easy access to smart society, he didn't seem to care what people thought of him. He had been to their schools and been expelled from them, ran up serious debts while serving as a commissioned officer in the army, and was 'a very naughty boy' (according to Lytton Strachey's friend, Dadie Rylands) while at King's College, Cambridge. When we met him at Deal he was beginning to satirise this world in his *Alms for Oblivion* sequence of novels (in which he is reputed to have used Philippa for the character of Maisie).

What we said that evening to give Philippa the genesis of her book, I do not exactly know. Nor did we know then, since she could never explain it. She hated being asked what her book was about. 'Actually, I do not know what the book is about,' she would volunteer. It was as if she were working at a gigantic jigsaw without a picture, and would see this picture for the first time in its entirety only when she put in the last piece.

Her starting point was food, the food and other appetites of the Victorians in relation to our own. 'I was unequipped to use standard analytical processes,' she later admitted. But she also thought that these analytical processes, when used by economists, for example, were unsatisfactory because they never followed the arguments into adjacent areas that bordered on their own speciality. In place of this truncated matter, Philippa wanted something all-embracing, which meant that she could not simply begin with the Victorians. 'I went deeper and further back into history until at last I arrived at the Roman Empire . . .'

Each day she set off for the Reading Room at the British Museum, determined to get a grounding in European history. She read and took notes, it seemed to me, on everything under the sun: agriculture, aphrodisiacs, social taboos, religious practices, eunuchs, witches, and of course the facts and figures of modern factory farming. With these researches she combined her own experiences, 'rummaging through hedgerows, wallowing in spices, pot herbs, puptons, pickles, jellies, fritters, ragouts and custards, bubbling mediaeval potions, tasting such rarities as messes of potage, frumenty, civet, charlotte, wild carrot, glasswort and skirret'. Some of these substances appear in her appendix of rare Roman and medieval recipes, others in an appendix about aphrodisiacs (called 'The Stuff of Dreams').

I watched this process with amazement and apprehension. Philippa worked, with terrible energy, to a point of exhaustion and with desperation, as if her life depended on it – as perhaps it did. I could help a little this time, giving her anecdotes and episodes that provided useful connective tissue in the narrative. 'Her study in Barnes, overlooking the back garden, was piled with the notes of her curious researches,' remembers Mike Foss, who had by then become a professional historian. 'Such was her enthusiasm for the ingenuity, and daring, of the human capacity for enjoyment that she drew others into her exhilarating chase. I thought I had no particular interest in her subject, but still found myself willingly digging about on her behalf in the Public Record Office.' He was obliged to gather dictionaries and grammars around him, for she put him and Simon Raven to work translating pages of Latin for her. So there, among the acknowledgements to several learned butchers of Deal, to Lloyds Bank in West Kensington, the editor of the *Meats Trade Journal*, the Federation of Women's Institutes and to Penelope Jardine 'for many scholarly errands in Rome' (where she met and spent the next thirty to forty years with Muriel Spark), stand their two names, Mike Foss and Simon Raven, both masters of Latin texts. '*Consuming Passions,* as the book was called, was my education,' she later wrote. 'My mind must be one of the most cumbersome and corroded that has ever tried to make a book. It was nerve-racking.'

But it succeeded – she succeeded. She reinvented herself in *Consuming Passions*, created a new life. When it was published in the autumn of 1970 (the publisher at the last minute replacing on the jacket a loaf of bread shaped like an extended penis with a respectable Hogarthian orgy), she was invited to appear on television to cook a medieval banquet. Her optimism leapt over the impossibilities, and the studio echoed with everyone's laughter – the crew, even the cameraman, could not stop laughing. At the end, the television presenter Eamonn Andrews sat down to taste her array of dishes – the 'furminty with venyson', 'Sir Kenelm Digby's White Pot', the 'goos in bogepotte' or 'harys in cyueye' – and as the end music began, the credits rose, he could be seen clutching his throat with a cry of 'Oh my God!' Then everything went blank. It was excellent television.

So what is her book about? It is about agricultural fertility rites and Anglo-Saxon drinking competitions, cheeses carried by the crusaders, joke food, severed heads, visions produced by fasting, remedies used in monasteries against ennui, surefire birth-control drugs in ancient Rome, the voluptuous menus of the Hell Fire Club, and Sweet Fanny Adams. You can find birds flying out of pies there, discover the medieval price of poultry and the fifteenth-century attitude to milk, and improve on the art of masturbation using vegetables (do not omit the well-endowed carrot). All this, and very much more, whirls around this extraordinary book. It is like a solar system, apparently chaotic yet with the abiding pattern of chaos, held together by a tremendous force of energy and inquisitiveness. Out of muddle and despair, with a prodigious effort of will, she had produced the most original and macabre creation. 'It is a work of love and care and art,' wrote *The Times* reviewer. 'Never have I come across such a crisp, exciting – such a very feminine history of taste.' Philippa dedicated it to me, and to me it remains a wonder.

Even before *Consuming Passions* was published, she had begun another book, her Life of Frank Harris.* This was at my suggestion, and she wrote it to some extent in tandem with my own work. My first biographical subject, Hugh Kingsmill, had written a brilliant memoir of Harris, who also had a good walk-on part in my *Augustus John* (and would later have a more significant role in my *Bernard Shaw*). I also possessed some Harris material left to me on his death by Hesketh Pearson (who had written two little-known essays on Harris).

All this made for a good start, and we took off on an enjoyable research tour through France, following Augustus John's journeys† early in the century until we arrived at Nice where, in 1907, John and Harris had an explosive encounter (we offered slightly different interpretations of it in our two books). Then we went on to Monte Carlo. I drove up to see

---

*In 2001 both *Consuming Passions* (with an afterword by Paul Levy) and *Frank Harris* were brought back into print in the Penguin Classic History and Classic Biography series.

†Philippa makes a brief, anonymous appearance in the preface to *Augustus John*, where she is shown enlivening some complicated negotiations at the Musée Rodin in Paris: 'a girl, indispensable I hoped to the pursuit of John scholarship, who was afflicted in several languages with an ingenious grasp of malapropism ("masturbate" for "masticate" was one I remember with affection).'

my stepfather Edy's grave on the Grand Corniche at La Turbie and also the tiny villa where my mother had taken me sometimes in the summer holidays from school. Philippa went to the Palace where she hoped to find something significant in the archive about Harris's friendship during the 1890s with Princess Alice of Monaco, an American forerunner to Grace Kelly. Palace protocol appeared strict, but after presenting formal letters of introduction from Captain Simon Raven MA (Cantab), late of the King's Shropshire Regiment, a Fellow of the Royal Society of Literature Michael Holroyd, as well as her well-hyphenated, Old-Etonian publisher, Christopher Sinclair-Stevenson – and finally, as a trump card, her three-guinea membership card of the Royal Horticultural Society – she passed muster and gained entry into the private archive. She was allowed to work there for only two days, as there was to be a royal festivity afterwards and all work must stop. She arrived at the Palace library as it opened and left when it closed, accidentally putting a bulging confidential file in her commodious bag and carrying it off on her last day. The rumpus this caused as, among the prancing horses, the marching soldiers, she struggled next morning to return the secret papers (spilling them over the parade ground in the wind) would make a fine scene were any film to be made of her life.

Readers of her *Frank Harris* will see that there is no acknowledgement or reference made to the Palace Archive at Monte Carlo. This was one of the Palace conditions – they did not wish to court further embarrassments. Those who are versed in biographical subtexts will become aware of an anomaly in Philippa's account of Frank Harris's relationship with Princess Alice and Prince Albert of Monaco. 'Harris's letters to Alice, together with all her papers, were by her wish burnt on her death by her executor Isador de Lara,' a footnote records. So what were the files on which she was working at the Palace, one of which she had briefly purloined? She makes no direct quotations from letters, but paraphrases passages when describing Harris's sentimental relations with Princess Alice and his dubious financial transactions with the Prince. This indirectness, however, becomes curiously appropriate for a man whose published memoirs, *My Life and Loves*, is so crowded with fantasy women, but who omits from it the women he actually knew.

Frank Harris was a good subject for Philippa. As one of her set pieces in *Consuming Passions*, along with Samuel Pepys's erratic breakfasts, Henry VIII's wedding celebrations and the pretensions of Trimalchio's Feast, she quoted Harris's dreadful account of a Lord Mayor's banquet, full of rotting green meat and accompanied by the pungent evacuations, delivered like pistol shots, of the Lord Mayor himself. But now her brilliant researches revealed much that had been unknown in Harris's miserable birth and upbringing, and which gave a background of pathos to his over-ambitious career. She exulted in some of his more outrageous exploits, but added compassion to high comedy. The man who boasted of knowing the King had actually longed to be invited by Mrs Humphry Ward to the house from which

Philippa as a schoolgirl had been expelled – she was sensible to such ironies. She also grew adept at distinguishing between Harris's wayward fantasies and the more modest facts of his life, because, she said, his compensatory stories were so like her own.

Philippa also came to liken Harris in her mind to Simon Raven. Both men, she believed, had once fallen in love, been rejected, and resolved never to be so fearfully hurt again. Neither of them dared to grow up, but inhabited clubs and institutions, like wombs, from which they were reluctantly ejected. Women they treated as fantasy creatures (Philippa had been to bed with Simon a few times for sessions of mutual masturbation but never thought of him as a lover). As they grew older, they lost touch with reality and came to believe their own fantasies. A parallel to Harris's lonely and disillusioned last years could, she later believed, be seen in Simon's last book, a memoir called '*Is There Anybody There?' Said the Traveller* (1990) in which she herself appears as 'a lank-haired authoress' much given to cooking 'blowflies, vervain and rabbit's sphincter', who mistakes a bottle of golden bath essence for some liqueur – a chartreuse, I think.

Philippa did not mind any of this, but she was appalled by the book's unkindness to her friend Guy Nevill who was dying of AIDS. Like Harris's last writings, the pages of Simon's final book seemed to her corroded with the bitterness of male impotence. Though he had enjoyed a new lease of his professional life by successfully adapting for television Trollope's six Palliser novels, as well as books by Nancy

Mitford, Aldous Huxley and Iris Murdoch, then writing *Edward and Mrs Simpson*, he did not appear to value this work. His charm evaporated, leaving a sourness lingering in the thin air. So their long, intermittent friendship stuttered to its end.

Cruelty was ever her enemy. Antagonism had entered our own relationship through the door of insanity. In madness, and in my sullen opposition to madness (the unhelpful, self-protective shell where I took cover), terrible things had been said that still hung mutely in the air we breathed. We had damaged each other so fundamentally that we could not repair ourselves. Our wounds remained as painful bruises that came vividly alive whenever small differences arose. When Philippa went off to the United States to study the Frank Harris papers held in several manuscript libraries there, I realised guiltily how grateful I was for the peace and freedom of her absence. When she returned, she told me I had missed an excellent opportunity for leaving and been a fool not to go. So, when she set off on a second tour of the United States, I did go, moving to a small flat in Fulham which I rented from a remarkable Swedish woman, Viveka Stjernsward, a friend of Elspeth Huxley. Here I struggled with the final chapter of *Augustus John*, his last illness and death, which I finished very slowly, feeling shell-shocked and empty. Then the typescript went away to its publisher, and I started a new life, happier at first, though leading to a tragedy.

After Philippa returned from the United States, she did not leave the house in Barnes for a month. She drank a great deal and then became crazily promiscuous. Stanley Olson,* who reported her as being under sedation, blamed my timing which, he told Frances Partridge, was a sign of my being 'emotionally immature'. There is perhaps no perfect moment for such a painful wrenching apart, and I do not think the timing was specially insensitive. But in so far as I felt unable to prolong the emotional battery, to move through the storms into calmer periods, the charge of immaturity may be true.

Six months after I left, Philippa went down with an

---

*Stanley Olson (1947–1989), the biographer of Willa Cather and John Singer Sargent (also appointed by Rebecca West as her authorised biographer) was an unforgettably perplexing character. Given up for dead at his birth in Akron, Ohio, by his parents, he later recreated himself in London as a striking English eccentric. Despite his natural awkwardness, dark spectacles and a somewhat cumbersome figure, he got himself up as a 1920s dandy, with clever bow ties, superbly tailored cream suits and startling co-respondents' shoes – in all of which he could be spotted pedalling his tricycle through the West End streets to the Ritz, his black spaniel Wuzzo alert in his special dickey designed at Harrods.

Stanley seemed to me the perpetual student, curious about everything, confusing about almost everything, knowledgeable and naïve, invalidish yet full of energy, generous and demanding, immature, precocious, affluent yet perpetually in debt, secretive, gossipy, a partial dyslexic determined to emerge as a fluent writer. In my imagination he appears as an amphibious creature rolling merrily, tragically, across the land, his adopted land, in thrall to the operas of Wagner and the survivors of Bloomsbury (he had written a thesis on the Hogarth Press). Eventually I found his hospitality too oppressive – I simply could not keep up. Stanley never seemed to sleep: then, at the age of thirty-nine, he suffered a paralysing stroke from which he eventually died. His biography by Phyllis Hatfield, *Pencil Me In*, was published in 1994 (André Deutsch).

undiagnosed illness. 'My temperature rose and stayed at about 103 degrees for about three weeks,' she wrote. 'Pints of sour yellow sweat poured out of me, day and night. The sheets were so wet they could literally be wrung out. When I recovered, my depression had more or less left me for ever . . . I felt light and euphoric.'

She was looked after by the improbable, larger-than-life figure of Paul Levy, the American writer, apricot-coloured, curly-haired, clever, secretly vulnerable, an out-to-lunch Kentucky Falstaff, bursting with generous fantasies, whom I had first met at Harvard in 1968. He had come to me after a lecture I delivered there and asked whether I could give him introductions to some surviving members of the Bloomsbury Group. Within a year, he was living in England and knew more people in and out of Bloomsbury than I did. One evening at dinner, he explained to me that his career stood at an agonising crossroads: should he write a masterpiece or become a professional gigolo? It was a knotty decision which he ingeniously untied by publishing his biography of the Cambridge philosopher and guru of Bloomsbury, G. E. Moore, and then changing course to become himself a philosopher in the kitchen. Living on a duke's estate, his raw fantasies were trodden into intoxicating fact.

During his first few years in England, Paul's life seemed to be shadowing my own so faithfully that Philippa suggested, as a joke, that he was secretly in love with me. In the early 1970s, after my *Lytton Strachey* was published, Paul edited Strachey's occasional writings in a volume called *The Really Interesting Question;* and while I was working on my

My Aunt Yolande in the 1920s

Yolande on holiday *c.*1935

Haselhurst *c.*1940
(see page 233)

Yolande at home, and (below) the inscription I chose for her

The author of *Mosaic* (*photograph © by John Foley*)

Philippa: while writing *Frank Harris* (left) and in the year of her death, 1997 (see page 166)

An unlikely couple: Maggie and Michael *c*.2000 (*photograph by Caroline Forbes*)

Reggie Beaumont-Thomas with his smart car and formidable mother

'Maimie' and 'Medal'

Agnes May and her younger sister Melville Pretoria, ready for a fancy-dress party *c.*1915

Agnes May: the hand-painted photograph commissioned by my grandfather
*c.*1928

biography of Augustus John, Paul hitched up with one of Augustus's granddaughters whom he would bring to Philippa's parties. Then, when I left her house in Barnes, Paul stepped in temporarily and, with his great energy and generosity, helped Philippa over a critical time. Later I was able to repay some of his kindness by facilitating his marriage to the art editor Penny Marcus, whom I had known quite well when she worked for the Tate Gallery. At their wedding party near Oxford, a splendid affair of tents, fireworks and celebrities, Paul appeared dressed entirely in white, while Penny, famous for her beautiful bones and soft voice, was in deepest black.

Philippa and I kept away from each other, not from enmity so much as cautious self-preservation. Soon I went west to live in Ireland (strategically placed between a convent and a barracks) to begin writing my biography of Shaw, travelling to the United States to work on Shaw's papers; Philippa went east on the first of several long journeys to India, where she fell under the spell of the boy guru Sai Baba, about whom she wrote in her 'spiritual travelogue', *The Shortest Journey*. She went on to study yoga and Sufism, began training with the National Federation of Healers and became an intuitive therapist, employing a bewildering range of techniques, from drumming to the laying on of hands. With the psychic teacher Lilla Bek, she was to write books on spiritual and lay healing, and also study Egyptian hieroglyphs with the passion she had previously brought to the study of European history in the British Museum. But she 'never fell for the whole spiritualist package', Paul Levy observed. Indeed she seemed

145

incapable of treating any religious enterprise with solemnity. She diverted an expedition to find the resting place of Noah's Ark on Mount Ararat with an excursion to see the swimming cats of Lake Van; she broke off her astrological researches into the Hindu religious fair, the Kumbha Mela, to write an article on dustbins; and she several times interrupted her studies in Egyptology at the University of London by leading parties of Temple Medicine Tours along the Nile – in the wake of which came streams of improbable 'Carry On' stories.

At last we began to see each other again. From time to time from the early 1980s onwards, Philippa would telephone me, ostensibly on matters of grammar: how to give linguistic support perhaps to some intimations of immortality arising from her transcendental meditation. Using many full stops, I would try my best. Then we would relax and have supper together. She was an inspired if eclectic cook (her curious green tomato crumble was well known for its psychedelic side-effects), and she still drank plenty of wine, some of it homemade. Was she using these exercises in transcendental grammar to release me from my male prison of rationality? Not seriously, I think, though she enjoyed making fun of me. She knew that I believed her to be advancing, like Frank Harris, ever further into fantasy. Instead of denying this, she would point out that fantasy was an everyday ingredient of our lives, and therefore part of reality. She also quoted Hugh Kingsmill back at me, to the effect that incredulity was no more adequate as a response to life than credulity. She lived somewhere between the two.

In fact I believed something rather different about the nature of her quest. She did not look after herself, fearing illness, doing nothing, simply waiting for it to pass, as men do. She preferred the idea of psychic to surgical operations. While travelling in the Philippines, she had fallen ill but ignored the symptoms, drank a lot until at last she lay dying on the beach, almost unconscious, finally it seems reconciled to death. But then she was rescued and taken to hospital, revived, operated upon (having her cancerous womb removed) and, regaining consciousness, was suddenly terrified of dying. She attributed the shock of this experience to a combination of alcohol and anaesthetics. In any event, the sudden apprehension of death, intense and awful, brought back to her, I believe, the feelings she had tried to suppress after her fiancé Robin died. This time she reacted differently. Much of what she hoped to find in her searches, and to give others, was a magic cocktail, inducing the courage of acceptance rather than forgetfulness, and lessening the horror and sadness of death. For unless it could be appeased, death came to us like a monstrous dragon from a child's nightmare. She had seen the devil in her madness; she wanted to become aware of a primordial and beneficent presence in the days of her well-being. What she possessed, and suggested that other people possessed, was a remarkable ability to change. At her house in Barnes, she created something like a temple to which all who were afflicted as she had been, all who were heavy-laden, could come: there was a priest, an analyst, a vet, an Irish painter, a secret drug-taker from the United States, a duchess, a harpsichordist, a transsexual, an astrologer, a divorcée, a man found nearby in a gutter, a woman who had made a comparative study of communion wines; there were alcoholics, men and women who were bereaved, the lost and fearful, wounded souls of all ages, classes, nationalities, conditions. She had lost her own womb, but made her house into a womb where these people felt they could be reborn. She was their Mother. Someone special. Some of them were excruciating bores, but it didn't matter. She lit candles and set them drumming, dancing, singing, praying, drinking, meditating, laughing. She gave them concerts and counselling. She gave them a good time so that they could gain more confidence, learn or remember how to take pleasure in life. They talked of Tantra, sorcery, Satanic possession, vasectomy, schizophrenia, magic mushrooms, garlic and samphire, magnetism, illusion and delusion, and the need to discover a synthesis of fact and fantasy, death and life within the great paradox of time. It was a house of imagination and healing pantomime.

Of contemporary politics Philippa knew almost nothing. Her world and that of party politicians had little in common, and what little there was they saw differently. Most politicians would not have liked her attitude, which was a form of *noblesse oblige*, while she deplored their tendency to narrow careerism, their poverty of imagination. In her own work she was helped for a time by a peer of the realm who performed some secretarial duties for her (and after whom, title and all, she named one of her cats). 'Like many with a naturally aristocratic temperament, she was egalitarian at heart,' observed Mike Foss. 'I think she would have agreed with Mandeville's *Fable of Bees*, liking not only the ironic mockery of the economic analysis but even more the wit and verve of disreputable ideas. She was nothing if not an iconoclast.'

Some people, such as Frances Partridge, always felt Philippa to be 'maddening' – and certainly she could be provocative. But Frances, I believe, resented the fascination Philippa exerted over several male friends they had in common – Paul Levy and Stanley Olson, besides myself. In much the same spirit she castigates in her diaries that other Bloomsbury translator from the French, Lucy Norton, a splendid Grand Duchess of a figure whom Frances casts as an 'arch-spider' weaving her web around me and Paul Levy. 'How can they bear to be deluged in the thwarted maternal feelings from that vast, cushiony bosom?' she asks with disgust.

Philippa must have sounded more purely eccentric to Frances, less easy to cast as a thwarted mother or malicious daughter, but whose irrational lurches towards self-destruction might destroy us all. She was undoubtedly a complex and difficult girl – that is what her parents thought, and also what others who knew her, cared for her, loved her, were sometimes driven to feel in her twenties and thirties. But then, at a point of crisis, she had turned and found a way of coming to terms with these threatening complexities. She, who had been rejected by her father, was to welcome the world's rejects into her home, turning conventional failure into a story of eccentric success. Her very difficulties became the source of her strength. She appeared to be congratulating

149

people on their problems and disabilities, as if they were special gifts that added to the rich variety of life and the entertainment of those parties that raged through the beautiful chaotic rooms of her house. The vitality of these amazing evenings buoyed everyone up. It was all right after all. Everything was all right, after all, in the end. Everything.

Philippa did not eliminate her riotous past, but added objects from this new phase in her life, her last phase, to the décor of her house which reflected all the stages of her strange pilgrimage.

A few of her old friends found it difficult to keep in step with her. 'Her stride was wayward. She went where she wanted. I drifted away not for lack of affection, but under the tyranny of circumstances,' recalled Mike Foss. 'I never saw her again.

> But from time to time, returning to south London, I cut across Barnes Common and passed the end of her old road. It looks much the same now as in those cheerful days – a slightly dingy tunnel of untrimmed vegetation leading to the abodes of the professional classes. Then, remembering Philippa, I cannot help but smile as I think of that unconstrained package of vivacity and candour – a radiant cuckoo in those nests of dullness.

My own life, which had been deeply thrust down, was then beginning a new and better phase. I read about it – and so later on did Philippa – in a newspaper one Sunday in the autumn of 1982. What I read appeared highly unlikely. The newspaper reported that I had secretly married the famous novelist, Margaret Drabble. Could it possibly be true? This was what people telephoned all week to ask. At my publishers they were taking bets for and against, and my editor (who knew me well and betted against) rang me to find out whether she had won. I hesitated to tell her the truth.

The truth was that I had returned from Dublin in the late 1970s to live in the badlands of Ladbroke Grove. It was an awkward journey back. The banks in Ireland had gone on strike and closed for several months. My bank had thoughtfully presented me with a piece of paper that, they explained, would enable me to transfer everything in my account, pretty well all my capital, to a bank in England. Unfortunately this piece of paper, though quite large and rather impressive in appearance, had been drafted inexactly (the number not agreeing with the figures as spelt out) and in consequence no English bank would honour it. I felt like Neville Chamberlain waving that fragment of paper signed by Hitler and proclaiming in 1938, 'Peace in our time.' Suddenly, in my own time, I had no money at all. And I had no peace of mind. I was bankrupt. I remember ringing the Dublin bank from London and speaking at some length to a woman there. She was very understanding, but could not help because, she eventually revealed, she was merely the cleaner – no one else was coming in during the strike.

Then there was my car. In Dublin, whenever Ireland played England, the Irish crowds would celebrate or retaliate by dancing jigs and tangos on the top of my car which, as I looked out at it next day, resembled a new form of low-slung sports model. Eventually I managed to get round this hazard by replacing the English numberplates with Irish ones. This meant, however, after I drove back to England, that I would be stopped every few miles by the police who insisted on searching it and me for IRA weapons. My progress through the streets was curiously intermittent until, through lack of money, I came to a halt.

As if this were not enough, there was also trouble with my trousers. Before leaving Ireland I arranged for almost all my clothes to be cleaned, packing them straight into the car as I left – only to find when unpacking in England that I had the jackets of my suits, but that was all.

I was cutting a poor figure on my return. Taking pity on me, not for the first time, the novelist Angela Huth carried me off to dinner at the Ark Restaurant in High Street Kensington and hearing a couple at the next table talking about a flat they wanted to sell, I walked desperately over to them and bought it. Of course I went over to see it the next day. I think I would have bought whatever I had seen, but what I actually bought was what I wanted. It was what estate agents call a 'maisonette', and I acquired it without benefit of estate agents. How then to pay for it? Nineteen thousand pounds. I partly solved the problem by taking my piece of paper to an Irish bank in London where I had no difficulty in retrieving my approximate money. A few days later I was hanging up my jackets in my new home. And I was soon joined by Bernard Shaw, whose papers, books and other scholarly baggage arrived by truck from Dublin. I settled down for life, as it were: Shaw's life.

The area around Notting Hill was not then generally fashionable or expensive. No one had thought to make a glamorous film there – the only Notting Hill films I had seen were *Ten Rillington Place* about the celebrated murders of seven women (round the corner from my new home) by John Reginald Christie (excellently played by Richard Attenborough), and *Pressure*, about kids squatting in derelict houses. The place had made brief appearances in literature – as Arthur Machen's nightmare country, where all roads led to Goblin City, the ancient cemetery of Kensal Green with its white gravestones and shattered marble pillars, the birds above circling like vultures, a detested habitation of the dead; and as G. K. Chesterton's wilderness of bricks and mortar dominated by the tower of Campden Hill Waterworks, a kingdom to be defended by the Napoleon of Notting Hill against the advance of progress.

But it was Colin MacInnes, with his novels of the 1950s London underworld, who was to make the place truly notorious. He saw it as a drug-laden suburb of stagnation, bisected and enclosed by concrete precipices, sinister culs-de-sac littered with smashed bottles, truncated crescents going nowhere, and crossed by random lines of railway scenery and the dark margin of the canal 'where nothing floats except cats and contraceptives'. These crazy intersections created mean and awkward slum islands and brought them perilously close to the tree-lined streets of respectability, graded Victorian mansions with their trim tended gardens.

Rising above all this uneasy habitation stood the grim fortification of Wormwood Scrubs (the awful, Dickensian-named prison), also a neo-gothic, nineteenth-century hospital with its turret of discoloured brickwork, the monumental gasworks rising and falling like some vast lung machine, and the hopeless ugly tower blocks – vertical traffic jams of stacked-up people.

Twenty years after Colin MacInnes's *Absolute Beginners* was published, when I moved in, many deliberate improvements had been introduced – brightly coloured sports facilities, neat new housing trust villages, symmetrically planted roundabouts. Notting Hill riots were reorchestrated into the Notting Hill Carnival, though violence still haunted the atmosphere under the fresh paintwork, between the bursts of repetitive music, in the shadows late at night. Martin Amis was now our laureate. I occasionally saw him wheeling his baby from the off-licence. He found the sub-motorway culture, with its dense, haphazard tattoos of competing graffiti (the angry scrawls in Arabic lettering through which could still be seen the glimmering commandment of the Great Beast 666: 'Do What Thou Will Shall be the Whole of the Law') a rich hunting ground for his exultant scenes of moral anarchy. In his pages everyone is out at night robbing everyone else in primitive exercises of financial redistribution. I was robbed three or four times, though the burglars, adding injury to insult, found almost nothing worth the stealing (who, after all, wants books?). They fell back, like tired children, into pointless disorder, scattering Shaw's manuscripts, like random clues in a paperchase, from room to room. By the time Margaret came visiting, my maisonette was barricaded with locks and alarms.

I take credit for introducing Margaret to the wastes of Ladbroke Grove. We used to go on walks between the caravan people and snooker players under the motorway, passing mountains of burnt-out cars, and the bones of bicycles lying, like dismembered skeletons still tethered to the lamp-posts, along rows of dying pigeons in the gutters, to the violently painted, half-demolished Apocalypse Hotel (from which no traveller returns), its desperate customers in the *trompe l'oeil* paintings hanging crazily from its windows, never to escape. Some evenings, to the distant beat of reggae music, we would stroll across the dark patches of communal gardens, avoiding their slippery puddles of vomit, their glinting patches of shattered glass, reading the plastic police notices politely requesting information about local murders, the trees stuck with children's appeals for lost dogs or cats – hazardous landscapes of evil-smelling rubbish that moved menacingly in the wind. For anyone keen on observing social change in Britain in an extreme form, this was compelling territory, and Margaret was to use it dramatically in *The Radiant Way*,* the first novel she wrote after our marriage. Here, with its cramped and dismal terraces, its underpasses and tunnels lit with flickering neon lights, Notting Hill

---

*Fifteen years later, in *The Seven Sisters*, she gave the place, now with its modern oases of health clubs and silver Eurostar sheds, another, more contemporary, going over.

became a place of desolation and danger, patrolled at night by foxes and wild cats, and rat-faced people watching invisibly from their holes as you hurried along the shabby streets past those vandalised cars in any one of which, perhaps your own, may rest a dismembered head, wrapped in a piece of mutton cloth, its eyes staring, threatening to petrify you. To such a ghastly region had she been serenaded from the sunny uplands of Hampstead Heath, with its innocent children flying kites, its healthy joggers and keen footballers, its romantic memories of Keats and Shelley. I did this.

I had known Maggie, as I shall call her from now on, over many years, meeting her at parties as a casual friend. But all this changed one day after she saw me lunching near the British Museum, the table piled with proper vegetables, opposite the imposing atheist and secretary of the Shaw Society, Barbara Smoker. We sat at our meal serious-faced, correct, like two chess players, intent, bent forwards, occasionally moving a bowl of curry, some proteins or a glass of tap water, concentrating on matters secular and alphabetical. Though we were way beyond reproach, something about this scene sent a pang of pity through Maggie's tender heart, and that evening she telephoned and invited me next week to join a dinner party she was giving at her house in Hampstead. I eagerly accepted, and when I drove away that night, I apparently left my raincoat in the hall – an act which may be seen as the equivalent, literary critics tell me, of the Victorian lady carelessly dropping her handkerchief.

By the beginning of the 1980s I was living quietly islanded off Ladbroke Grove, still with Bernard Shaw, behind my double glazing and grilles. And though I still invited emotional complications, in some ways I lived simply and, despite the paraphernalia which made it more difficult for me to go out than for burglars to get in, I had little of the siege mentality of some war children. 'Apart from books,' Maggie reported after an early visit, 'there wasn't much else in his house. The fridge contained a lemon, bottles of white wine, vodka and mineral water. There were withered walnuts in a jewel box, a small can of baked beans in a cupboard, and an oven without a door . . . I know Michael can survive on bananas.' With these bananas, and little else, I apparently resembled the eponymous figure in *Krapp's Last Tape*. But I had a future.

The marriage took everyone by surprise. After all, was I not a happy-go-lucky bachelor, more eligible for affaires than weddings? By then I was getting on for fifty, and could go no more a-roving. And hadn't Maggie sworn never to remarry following her divorce ('a painful process best forgotten') from the talented actor Clive Swift? But like Philippa, she was one of the last of the Early Marriage Generation who married to get away from their mothers. Up to the mid-1980s, a woman's career was not generally accepted as a fit reason for leaving home. But marriage, however implausible, had to be accepted.

It was reported, our marriage, as a very bold enterprise, but it was in fact more of a tentative experiment. We experimented first by taking a trial-and-error honeymoon well before the wedding, setting off together for a week in

Hollywood where we saw the first night of Christopher Hampton's play *Tales from Hollywood.* Back in London we continued going out and staying in together and then spent an enchanted summer in Somerset, where Maggie had rented a somewhat derelict Dower House (the bed we slept in collapsed in the first week and we passed the following weeks sleeping on the floor). The house lay in a lost valley where the sheep were all pink from the red earth, the sun sank early behind the tall hills, and time itself seemed magically suspended.

Our experiment in courtship continued that summer in my blue, automatic car in which I taught Maggie to drive, chiefly by falling asleep in the passenger seat next to her – a gesture of confidence in her ability to steer us safely home at night. She always did. 'I must have been in some kind of trance all that summer,' she admitted. 'We were captives to one another and the driving lessons were our alibi.'

We were married in September 1982 at the Chelsea Register Office in the King's Road. Beryl Bainbridge acted as our 'best man', and the function was conducted by a forbidding lady in black whose bunch of keys, jangling from her waist, brought unpleasantly to mind the word wedlock. When she told us we should have gathered more witnesses, I brightly suggested going to the romantic fiction shelves of the public library next door and recruiting a few devotees there. She was severely unamused.

The most shocking ingredient of the marriage, to judge from later press coverage, was our decision to keep our two homes. Maggie's house in Hampstead was full of the coming-

and-going of teenage children (she had two sons and a daughter), a visiting mother, and an assistant who was working with her every weekday on the commodious *Oxford Companion to English Literature*. As for me, Bernard Shaw now occupied two of my three rooms and the avalanche of his words was leading to the subsidence of the building. So our arrangement was really one of romantic common sense. We spent weekends in Hampstead and had dinner together two or three times a week, telephoning each other whenever we were apart. We also took holidays and went on lecture tours abroad together. Had we not been married we would have been described as 'living together' by journalists who, since we were married, reported us as living apart.

We had hoped to keep our marriage relatively private so that, as stale news, it became no longer 'newsworthy'. But after two or three weeks, it was reported in the *Sunday Times*. What exercised journalists, then and thereafter, was these *deux ménages*. What could it all mean? What it meant was that the institution of marriage was changing, becoming more varied and less constraining than it had been thirty years earlier. Privately people understood this, and many couples envied our freedom and intermittent distance. But publicly our arrangement was represented as deeply unconventional, dubious and eccentric. In vain did I try to explain that most couples had homes from home that were called offices, whereas we worked at home and needed more space there. As eminent predecessors I cited William Godwin and Mary Wollstonecraft living as near neighbours after their marriage. Eventually my statements grew more whimsical. I explained that I had been studying Hugh Kingsmill's famous panorama on marriage, *Made on Earth* (1937), and been influenced by Milton's good-natured views on divorce. I very much liked too, I added, the Shavian notion of limiting the marriage contract (easily obtainable from the drugstore) to one year, with a joint option to renew it every twelve months. It was left to Maggie to translate my concoction of references and quotations into understandable language. Marriage did not suit everyone, she reminded astonished listeners, and it had to be handled with care. It should no longer be an expectation or an obligation. Perhaps the only odd feature of our own marriage, it occurred to her, was me. 'He invents things as he goes along. This is very liberating.' It was also a great compliment, I decided, for a non-fiction writer.

Though I had told some friends about our marriage, and also my parents (who had never met Maggie), I had not yet told Philippa, who eventually read about it in a newspaper. Our own stormy relationship ten or twelve years earlier had made me wary of letting anyone know much of my sexual and emotional life. I kissed and did not tell. For how could you tell anything of significance without introducing betrayal? The answer to that perhaps is that it can only be done in the calm distance of retrospect, as I am attempting to do – and even then the telling is like a difficult translation from another language, from privacy into print.

Philippa did not compartmentalise her life as I did. She packed everything and everyone together – and let them all sink or swim. In her more riotous past people had sunk, and there were genuine regrets. But now, by whatever inflatable means, they stayed afloat.

Philippa wanted to meet Maggie and in due course invited us to supper in Barnes. As we drove across the Common and along the pot-holed private road to the house where I had lived in the very late 1960s and early 1970s, I attempted to carry on introducing her to Maggie before they met. Their personalities, background, lives and careers were so thoroughly dissimilar that I could not imagine what they would make of each other, how they would get on. Yet I very much wanted them to get on, rather in the manner of the dying Edward IV in Shakespeare's *King Richard III*, urging those around him to be at peace so as to facilitate his own passage into heaven: 'Hastings and Rivers, take each other's hand/ . . . Dorset, embrace him; Hastings, love lord marquis/ . . . And make me happy in your unity.'

We parked between the pot-holes, struggled through the overgrown front garden past an enormous wooden statue of a naked woman, knocked and pressed bells, and heard the collective mewing and scampering of the animals within. Then footsteps, some rattling of the doors, cries of despair over keys – and we were in. I immediately put on an abstracted air as if I were partly elsewhere, at least not all there, wandering vacantly around and bumping into misplaced furniture until given something useful to do: the pouring of drinks. Then I waited to see what course the evening would take.

Philippa and Maggie had only one thing in common that they knew – and that was me (though perhaps I was a slightly different person with each of them). Since my return from Ireland and move into Ladbroke Grove, Philippa had developed an attitude of affectionate teasing towards me. Maggie at once picked up on this, and in relief perhaps I played along with it. But what on earth did Maggie really think? 'I liked Philippa immediately,' she later told me,

> though I could not have said why, and liked her more and more as I got to know her better. Indeed I think I came to love her.
>
> I can hear her voice now – she had pronounced and endearing vocal mannerisms, a kind of lilting precision, a strange and musical distribution of emphasis that I found very attractive. Her manner was calm, but at the same time intense and attentive ...
>
> She was full of stories – about handsome men and Arab stallions in Egypt, about Egyptian mythology, about stars and flowers and potions. I suppose Philippa was whimsical, in that she was full of whims, but she was sharp and witty, not sentimental. She was a risk-taker with a great and fearless openness, and a rare adventurousness of spirit. Most people who talk about calm and healing (not that she did, much) make me feel very tense, disbelieving and irritable, but Philippa had the reverse effect. She did calm and heal people. She was the real thing.

I could see, too, that Philippa warmed to Maggie, who was far from being the didactic literary intellectual she had feared,

and in fact something of an open-minded bohemian herself
with a soft spot for risk-takers and romantics, the
dishevelled, even the destroyed. Philippa invited herself down
to Somerset, and us to a tumbledown house she had rented
on Valencia Island off the west coast of Ireland while we were
over there one year. I remember her giving us strange,
delicious, green drinks that produced, over the following
week, unfortunate effects on my driving. Not a day passed
without my losing, by some infinitesimal miscalculation, a
couple of wing mirrors, some bumpers, the aerial and so on
until, by the time we reached mid-Wales on our way back to
England, I was driving a skeleton car as if in a cartoon. But
mostly I remember our visits to her house in Barnes. And so
does Maggie.

She seemed to lead a charmed life, in a charmed place.
I was very impressed by the beautiful and luxuriant
disorder of the house – large high rooms, with large
paintings, and large mirrors and dark comfortable
furniture. There was a feeling of faded grandeur, as
though we were in an old much-inhabited country
house in town, where the same people and animals
had been living for generations ... There were cats
everywhere, weaving their way along mantelpieces,
sitting toasting themselves on the Aga, curled up before
log fires, disappearing crossly down dark corridors.
There was one particular cat called Mr Parsley whose
name gave me much delight. There were also fish.
Philippa had made an indoors-outdoors fishpond

conservatory, and in the pond large golden fish teemed and proliferated. They came to her call, like chickens.

It is hard to make friends later in life, but here, it seemed to me, was a genuine late friendship. To some extent I was its catalyst – they both put themselves out for my sake – but then it developed its own momentum irrespective of me. They held unlikely interests – I remember them one dark night in the middle of Barnes Common, their heads raised to the heavens, identifying clusters of stars. Another night, after they had been out walking, Maggie fell asleep on the hearthrug. 'I am not very good at falling asleep on other people's hearthrugs, so Philippa must have cast a spell on me,' she later explained. 'She did have a magic quality.'
They trusted each other, made the other feel she was doing the right thing, were discerningly uncritical, spontaneously generous, and made me happy in their unity. That was the magic. At Christmas, or on a birthday, Philippa would sometimes lead small troops of her friends on rustic-suburban walks, animating the landscape around them with surreal visions. I remember Maggie coming back and telling me of a field of llamas near Guildford, and a red-haired woman praying on her knees near a chapel. These walks would end in celebratory parties at Barnes, where I had been left in charge of the oven and cats.
There were many gaps between our meetings, since all of us were working hard and quite frequently travelling. After her mother died, Philippa became rather more secluded, listening to her radio in the evenings and working on her patchwork quilt.

In some ways she was not so unlike her mother, possessing a similar stubbornness and individual tastes (Mrs King enjoyed drinking a bottle of stout over a meal, followed by some sweet wine). She had by this time reached the age at which the thoughts turn lightly towards family history. She was delighted to find, hidden in the dark past, a spirited ancestor called Dolores, a dancer from Spain, her great-great-something-or-other, who married an Irishman and produced a daughter who had connections with Edinburgh Gaol. Much encouraged, she travelled north to pursue her investigations and was rewarded by the discovery of a scandal involving 'the MacDonald of Sleat'. It was all most promising, though it took her out of London a great deal. One summer – it was in 1997 – we noticed that we had not seen Philippa for more than six months, and I rang to invite her over to Ladbroke Grove. She answered hesitantly, saying that she expected to be off on a long journey soon, a sort of holiday. I told her she must see us when she came back.

Six weeks later she was dead. She had told almost no one that she was suffering from terminal lung cancer. She was looked after by a homeopath doctor and a practitioner of aromatherapy and reflexology who gave her massages to relieve her laboured breathing. She was determined not to die in hospital. In *The Times* obituary, Paul Levy wrote: 'She refused treatment, saying that she would take upon herself the responsibility for her illness – either healing it or managing her own death. In either case she intended to set an example for the many people she had nurtured and helped, and with the minimum of drugs she did just that, fortified by the essentially comic view of life that is evident in all her books.'

With this obituary appeared an extraordinary photograph of her taken in the last year of her life. It shows a face of confrontation and acceptance, with signs of pain absorbed into it, as she sits, a shawl round her shoulders, waiting. She has a determined expression, not grim but with nothing weak or trivial in it. I find it almost unbearably moving.

Her younger son Sebastian, whom I had first got to know in Deal, telephoned to tell us the news and we went over for the last time to her house in Barnes. Brilliant sunshine filled the garden and gave a dusky warmth to the rooms. Her body still lay in the bedroom upstairs before eventually being taken to Shropshire for its dedication and green burial in 'a lush green valley, full of bird chatter and animal life'.*

---

*Philippa had made it clear that she wanted her body to be put in a cardboard coffin and buried in a place of natural beauty. The Natural Death Centre (to which she was attached as a spiritual healer) held a list of approximately seventy such sites, and was able to help her son Sebastian find a cardboard coffin and also give him the information he needed for an embalming service. The site he chose outside Ludlow belonged to Ann Dyer, who was offering her ancient orchard for private burials and who intended to plant it with memorial apple trees whose species were under threat. An additional advantage to this site was the Dyer family chapel, on the edge of the orchard, where Philippa's Celebration of Life service was held on Sunday 14 September 1997.

About twenty-five of Philippa's friends wanted to go to this burial ground, and her aromatherapist, Viv Knowland, took on the job of getting a coach company which would be prepared to take them, along with Philippa's body in its cardboard container, into Shropshire. 'There were some very strange reactions to my request,' she recorded. '. . . [and] mutterings about the Health

Her friend Stella Wilkinson had noticed how her corpse had been changing over the days. At the beginning it had looked extraordinarily ancient, almost Egyptian, then more like a bird, and then again like a girl, an Ophelia, with long dishevelled hair spread out as if floating on water. 'I had never seen an unembalmed corpse before or experienced the shocking difference of flesh tone after life,' Stella said. 'It was part of her generosity not to have been a frightening corpse.' It was also perhaps due to the manner of her death. Many people, as the doctor confirmed, die in fear, leaving dreadful, contorted expressions on their faces. But Philippa had not died like this. The atmosphere in the house, though peculiarly intense at the start of her final illness (she did not like being nursed by her son), had, I was told, grown easy and serene as

---

& Safety Act.' Eventually she did find an owner and driver who, for £500, was prepared to drive everyone the three hundred miles or more from Philippa's house in Barnes to the orchard near Ludlow and back, with the coffin, now decorated with Egyptian symbols in shades of blue, terracotta and gold and lined with a roll of muslin, placed in the luggage hold underneath. Viv Knowland has described the day of 'Philippa's green and final journey'.

'We set about decorating the Chapel with flowers and candles in preparation for our service. Philippa's coffin was laid out in front of the altar with an amethyst crystal and her handmade drum placed on top of the coffin. The service was almost spontaneous with everyone taking part – there was chanting, prayers, remembrances, poetry, Irish flute music, Bible reading, a song specially composed and sung for Philippa, a period of contemplation and meditation – a wonderful mixture of happiness, sadness, smiles and tears . . .

'The coffin was then carried slowly across the orchard to the prepared grave. Bay leaf branches and rosemary sprigs were strewn over the bottom of the pit and then Philippa in all her splendour was lowered gently into the grave.'

her strength evaporated. And that tranquil atmosphere persisted after her death.

We sat in the garden, the unseen trains clattering by from time to time. This intermittent noise made a strange juxtaposition of two worlds, as Maggie later remarked, the muffled sound of the trains reminding her of another timescale, yet somehow intensifying the remote and rural quality of Philippa's world. I was touched by Sebastian's mild unworldliness. He seemed unprotected, but Philippa's spirit lived on in him, I felt. They had been peculiarly close over her last year and the sweetness of his temperament, reflecting this closeness, was very appealing. It looked as if he had got her love at last. He told me that his mother had finished her dissertation, *Magic and Mysticism in the Ancient Egyptian Pyramid Texts*, for an MA course at Kent University – she had corrected the proofs the day before she died. Then we relapsed into stories of Philippa's boisterous séances, and the time she had been likened to Joan of Arc after falling into Lord Montagu's fire at Beaulieu.

But her death had been untimely in many ways. There was much unfinished business especially in relation to her sons. The elder one, whom she had considered conventional, was to become a part-time chimney sweep. How she would have liked that – liked that in him.

While I talked with Sebastian, Maggie went and lay in the long grass under the mulberry tree. 'I felt a sense of great loss, as though something irreplaceable had been taken away – as indeed it had. The sun shone gloriously, the garden was still beautiful, the cats still weaving their way around, the flowers still clambering through all the open windows, and I knew that we would never enter this small paradise again.'

Then we left.

When first hearing of Philippa's death, Maggie had burst into tears, lamenting the loss of a friend in the future, the friend of old age she would miss. I sat with that numbness which is a refusal to believe, the first stage of a familiar grief which woke me early each morning, sat on me like a stone even before I had remembered the death that was its cause.

'It seems a senseless thing to die!' That line of verse which Philippa had used as part of an epigraph for her biography of Frank Harris came back to me. I got the book down and began reading. What particularly struck me was the last paragraph of her preface which is a restatement of Samuel Johnson's declaration in his *Life of Savage* that no one who has not suffered the same misfortunes and persecution as Savage has the right to judge him ('nor will any wise man presume to say, "Had I been in Savage's condition, I should have lived and written better than Savage"'). Philippa wrote:

It is tempting to feel ourselves more worthy, sympathetic and serious than Harris, to be disappointed with the facts of his life since they do not support the notion of him as the anti-Puritan hero that he longed to be. In this biography I have tried to show Harris as someone more human and complicated than either a hero or a villain. He was a man whose ambitions exceeded his talent and his energy. This is a condition that at one time or another has afflicted most of us and

169

calls for the kind of understanding that we would wish for ourselves.

That is the spirit in which I have tried, in response to Margaret Forster's challenge, to write about Philippa in this chapter. Have I answered her question? Perhaps not. But I have, I hope, imbued these pages with some of Philippa's talents and shown what she gave me – what I needed to be given.

Maggie and I do not speak much of Philippa now: she is part of our known and accepted pasts – part of our unspoken selves. But occasionally something will prompt another memory, make us speak it aloud. In *The Literary Companion to Cats*, Clare Boylan quotes some lines by Francis Scarfe:

Those who love cats which do not even purr
Or which are thin and tired and very old,
Bend down to them in the street and stroke their fur,
And rub their ears and smooth their breast, and hold
Their paws, and gaze into their eyes of gold.

I know those cats. They found sanctuary in Barnes and somehow they survive in the dangerous streets of Ladbroke Grove. Maggie waits patiently, with understanding, as I stop to stroke one of them. But then I hear Philippa's voice warning me not to deceive it into trusting all human beings. 'You don't want it made into gloves!' So I content myself by whispering this warning before going on.

In the garden at Somerset, Maggie suddenly recalls what Philippa said of a plant there (Teucrium maris) tumbling down a wall. 'It has such a pretty habit.' It is a phrase that regularly comes back to her now, 'because she herself had so many pretty and graceful natural habits'.

A more sombre note came from Robert Skidelsky. Relishing Philippa's 'great presence and many changes of style', he remembered last seeing her 'sitting, as it were, on a throne, improbably dressed like the Queen Mum'. But if Philippa, who called to mind such a symbol of longevity and was herself always fizzing with eccentric energy, could die so unexpectedly, and so comparatively young, then for the rest of us 'it's choppy water from now on'.

A tree was planted above her body in Shropshire. 'I sometimes pause and think of this tree,' writes Eduardo Sant'Anna, 'firmly rooted in the ground with its branches spreading through mid air, swaying from side to side almost in a frenzy, almost like someone I used to know.'

6

The Search

FAMILY STORIES

Pilgrim's Progress, about a man who left his family, it didn't say why.

Mark Twain, *The Adventures of Huckleberry Finn*

. . . here, where the living and the dead share the same space, sometimes, in order to find one of them, you have to make a lot of twists and turns, you have to skirt round mountains of bundles, columns of files, piles of cards, thickets of ancient remains, you have to walk down dark gulleys, between walls of grubby paper which, up above, actually touch, yards and yards of string will have to be unravelled, left behind, like a sinuous, subtle trail traced in the dust, there is no other way of knowing where you have to go next, there is no other way of finding your way back.

José Saramago, *All the Names* (translated by Margaret Julia Costa)

Among all the stories I was sent, there was nothing of the person about whom I was most eager to learn more: my grandfather's *femme fatale*, Agnes May. As I toured the country giving readings and talks about family memoirs at festivals, I would ask the audience if they knew anything of her, but answer came there none, and we usually settled for putting all our families into fierce competition as to which was the most dramatic, secret, dysfunctional, strange. Even abroad, in Chicago or Montreal, my own family performed very well in these contests.

After three or four months, I thought of a new way to elicit information, and drafted an article which I called 'A Tale of Two Women'. The two women were Agnes May and my Aunt Yolande. Looking closely at their very different lives, I saw that they represented a dramatic shift in the moral and sociological landscape of Britain. When things go wrong, as they did for my aunt, I wrote,

> we are tempted to ask who is to blame. But perhaps this is not the right question. In retrospect my Aunt Yolande's fate appears inevitable, as if it were locked into a national predicament, its narrative keeping pace with the decline in imperial and class confidence. The other side of that story is the wonderful rise in the fortunes of my grandfather's ex-working-class mistress, Agnes May.

I went on to expand this article into a public appeal for information about Agnes May, using facts I had discovered but been unable to work into the published narrative of my book. Perhaps it was not surprising that my grandfather's mistress had been only seven years older than his daughter. As I had presented her to the reading public, Yolande appeared like the character in an Anita Brookner novel, limited by cultural conditioning, perhaps also by loss of nerve or an excess of sensitivity, disappointed in her romantic expectations, left alone long before the end. Agnes May, on the other hand, was far from solitary and had the makings of a twentieth-century Becky Sharp. I longed to find out more about her.

'She had been born at 56 Hardshaw Street, St Helens, in Lancashire, a daughter of the glass-grinder Joseph Bickerstaff and his wife Robina (whose maiden name had been Laurie),' I explained in my article.

Unlike Yolande, who stayed so dutifully with her parents, she must have left St Helens before she was twenty – she was not yet twenty-one when she married Second-Lieutenant William Reynolds Lisle, at Oxted, near Godstone; and only in her twenty-first year when, eleven days after having been divorced, she married Captain Thomas George Symonds Babb, the son of a hotel proprietor in Minehead, Somerset . . .

Eight years later, Thomas Babb cited my grandfather as co-respondent in his divorce petition. Agnes May immediately married a wealthy businessman, Reginald Alexander Beaumont-Thomas, and went to live in Duchess of Bedford Walk, Kensington. *The London Street Directory* shows them living there for a couple of years. Then they vanish and the trail runs cold.

It had taken many weeks of research to trace her this far. I went to Minehead and advertised in the local paper there to find out if anyone remembered her or her second husband; I went to Oxted, had tea in Rose Cottage, Barrow Green Lane, where she had briefly lived with her first husband, and examined the deeds of the house (which appeared to belong to a railway company). But nowhere could I pick up an echo of her presence, the ripple of a distant memory. From all these places, including Kensington (where I examined old telephone books, the electoral register and street directories at the local studies centre) she had quickly moved on leaving, as it were, an empty page.

I consoled myself by reflecting how fortunate I had been to

locate her at all. Initially I knew nothing except what I learnt from a Deed of Covenant my grandfather made in the early 1930s when granting her a quarterly allowance for 'past services'. I came across this document at the back of a chest of drawers after my father died and saw that her name was then Agnes May Babb and that she was a married woman (the allowance ceased if she returned to her husband). With this meagre fact I went to the Registry of Births, Deaths and Marriages, then at St Catherine's House in the Aldwych, and began trawling through the apparently endless lists of marriages in their heavy alphabetical volumes. Had her husband's name been Smith or Jones, the hunt would have been impossible. But the surname Babb is comparatively rare and so, even if I did not then know her husband's first name, I always felt there was the prospect of discovering her. I looked backwards for the Babbs's marriage, and then I looked forwards to see if by any chance she had married again. Altogether I covered almost fifteen years of marriages throughout England and Wales: and then one afternoon I found her. She had married Reginald Alexander Beaumont-Thomas in 1934. Luckily their marriage certificate was crammed with information. It gave me her father's name, her age, the full name of her ex-husband and, then a surprise to me, the fact that this was her third marriage. A month later, by laborious trial and error, I had in my possession her three marriage certificates, her divorce papers from Somerset House, and her birth certificate. Yet I felt she was fighting me all the way. By continually experimenting with her age, changing her first names fantastically as well as her last, haphazardly inventing addresses for herself and wide-ranging professions for her father who regularly dies and miraculously comes alive again on these official papers, she had laid down such a thick smokescreen that I finally lost her. Had she married a fourth or even a fifth time? Had she gone to live abroad, perhaps in the United States or France, and then died there? She could not still be alive or, if she were, then she was nicely over one hundred years old. All things seemed possible, but the fact was she had given me the slip.

I switched my lines of enquiry first to her father's family, the Bickerstaffs, then to her last-known husband's family, the Beaumont-Thomases. Sometimes the quickest way to find the date of a death is to search through the inventory of Wills and Letters of Administration. I discovered that Joseph Bickerstaff, who died in Hampshire in 1942, left an estate valued at £207 which automatically went to his widow Robina. There was no mention of their daughter Agnes May, and Robina Bickerstaff herself left no will when she died the following year at Myrtle Cottage, Brockenhurst – probably, I thought, because she had no money. 'Like a bird, Agnes May appears to have freed herself from her family cage,' I concluded, '. . . [and] was moving in wealthy circles by then, in contrast to my Aunt Yolande who never married and remained financially dependent on her family all her life.'

I surmised that Agnes May must have been quite wealthy because of my investigations into the Beaumont-Thomas family. One of the more infuriating obstacles in research is the hyphenated name. Sometimes this family appeared simply as Thomas, at other times they shot up the alphabet and attained

Beaumont. In the hope that someone might remember them and respond to this appeal for information, I put into my article all I had discovered about Agnes May's third husband since finishing my book. The second son of a successful steel manufacturer, Reginald Beaumont-Thomas was educated at G. Davison Brown's preparatory school in Brighton, and went on to Eton College. His early years were deeply unmemorable. Despite getting through three tutors at Eton, 'he won no prizes, played no games, and left after only two years', I wrote after consulting the archivist at Eton College Library.

He was almost eight years younger than Agnes May, and this was not his first marriage, either. In Paris, at the age of twenty-two, he had married Germaine Blanche Aimée Dubor, who seven years later petitioned for a divorce on the grounds of his desertion. That year, 1932, he gives as his address the Junior Carlton Club in London. His name appears in the 1937 edition of *Burke's Landed Gentry* as the younger brother of Lionel Beaumont-Thomas, then living at Great Brampton, Madley, Herefordshire. But Reginald's marriage is not mentioned, and all the Beaumont-Thomas family disappear from future editions.

This article appeared in the *Sunday Times* in Britain, and *Threepenny Review* in the United States. I waited, apparently in vain, not knowing that it would eventually lead to an extraordinary discovery transferring my aunt from the solitary pages of an Anita Brookner novel to the crowded text of Iris Murdoch's fiction with its formations of elaborate coincidence and its complex infrastructure of relationships.

The first intimation I heard of something strange was during a telephone call from my friend Carmen Callil. She had dined earlier that week with some friends of her family, one of whom had seen my book and told her I had got everything wrong about my aunt's lover and fiancé, Hazlehurst. She had known him for the best part of forty years and never heard him speak of a Yolande Holroyd. Either I had got hold of the wrong man, or else my Aunt Yolande had been living out a fantasy affaire. On the whole it was probably the latter, she thought, since Hazlehurst was certainly a most fascinating man who mesmerised many people. But he was also a married man, eventually a much-married man. In these circumstances, it was highly unlikely that he had been so closely attached to my aunt and for such a long time – over ten years. Besides, it was not as if he were afraid of mentioning the names of women, particularly a woman called Iseult. Could this Iseult have been by any chance his pet name for Yolande?

I remember laughing at this far-fetched notion. After all, I had Hazlehurst's letters to my aunt spanning almost ten years, and in none of them did he call her Iseult, or anything but Yolande, his dear and beloved Yolande, the woman he hoped to marry once he had made enough money to propose and be accepted by her parents. On the envelope of an early letter my aunt misspelt his name. He wrote back at once from his yacht to correct her, spelling out his surname in capital letters at the top of his reply.

PS HAZLEHURST
   NOT HAZELHURST
CHISWICK 6343.   YACHT FROTHBLOWER,
                        ~~CUBITTS YACHT BASIN,~~
              C/o Turgh Bros · CHISWICK, W. 4.
                   ~~Teddington~~
                   ~~Saturday~~   9/9/33

Dearest one,

    I was so very glad to get your
letter. You were such a time answering
mine that I almost thought you were
taking me literally when I asked you not
to waste valuable time writing to me. As
you probably guessed from my last letter
not being frightfully fit I was a bit
depressed & the actual wait for the
postman still further depressed me. As
then I am I imagined all sorts of
things such as you finding someone
else, it wouldn't be difficult for you
you know. At any rate if men thought

But because he signed his love letters with a simple 'H', I never got to know his first name (everyone called him Hazel), and I was unable to find his birth certificate. So he remained something of a mystery to me – but not so mysterious that I could credit the stories of Carmen's friend.

Shortly afterwards, I received a rather impatient letter from a reader of my article, 'A Tale of Two Women'. She wanted to know whether the memories of my grandfather's mistress, Mrs Beaumont-Thomas, which she had sent me were of use. 'I should be most pleased to hear as naturally I am now very interested myself and could maybe help you further.' I was not surprised to find that the newspaper had failed to forward this correspondence. It had not treated my contribution as a genuine appeal for information and, greatly thickening the confusion, had shown a picture of my Aunt Yolande as if she were my grandfather's mistress, Agnes May. Fortunately, my correspondent had kept a copy of her original letter, marked 'Private and Confidential', which she now posted to me. This, too, questioned and pretty well refuted the story I had told in *Basil Street Blues*. 'My mother was a great friend of the Beaumont-Thomases,' my correspondent explained, remembering her visits to them in Brighton.

On occasions I would be taken to visit them on a Sunday morning for cocktails. She was called Vera and appeared far from a 'scarlet woman'. Slim, attractive, sophisticated with great style, always kind and warm to a gauche 16 year old boarding school girl. Reggie

[Beaumont-Thomas] was a paraplegic from an injury he sustained playing Rugby at Eton (I believe). He was tall, good looking, hospitable and charming. He was always in a wheelchair and she was caring and attentive – they seemed very fond of each other. They had no children and lived in a bungalow (for Reggie's chair, I assume). Vera drove the Rolls ... She was a delightful woman who obviously had to re-invent herself to escape the dreary working-class north and, after sorting out a few early mistakes, found happiness with Reg for around 40 years. And with a paraplegic, that has to be love.

Though this letter was full of oddities (such as playing 'Rugby at Eton'), I felt certain that here was the Reginald Beaumont-Thomas who married Agnes May in the mid-1930s. She was continually calling herself new names and inviting others to do so. But what did surprise me was the dramatic way in which she had continued to reinvent herself. That the daughter of a working-class glass-grinder from Lancashire should have fled south while still in her teens, married two husbands and lived with my grandfather (one of her 'early mistakes') in her twenties and early thirties, then landed up, while still in her thirties, marrying a millionaire was remarkable enough. But that she should then have changed from a 'scarlet woman' to this knitted figure of domestic virtue and connubial stamina – a very model of matronhood – took me aback. I had difficulty picturing her as a devoted nurse. Yet it appeared to be true.

The next letter from a reader was more contradictory still. Thomas Lyttelton remembered very well the phenomenal Mrs Beaumont-Thomas (known locally as 'Mrs B-T'). She was living in Highgate Village during the 1940s and until the early 1950s when she left London for East Anglia. Hers was an 'unforgettable name to me, so often was it repeated by my parents in my teenage years', he wrote.

> By no means devoid of 'character' themselves, my parents clearly saw their equal in Mrs B-T . . . A large, robust 60ish year old, as I just remember meeting her, living apparently alone in this huge house [where] . . . her name, perhaps spirit, lived on.

He then gives me that name (which she signed on the contract of sale for the house): Iseult Marjorie Beaumont-Thomas.

All at once the country appeared to be teeming with Mrs Beaumont-Thomases of various heights and widths, robust, scarlet or nurse-like, and in different places at the same time – all of approximately the same age. Yet I knew from my researches that there was only one Beaumont-Thomas family in Britain. I simply could not make sense of it.

Finding some sense in it all was made no easier by the number of false trails that were opening up, such as a picture of a high-spirited dancing lady, apparently in Hungarian costume and allegedly Agnes May in full bloom, that was sent to me from Dublin. Was this herself? On investigation, it turned out to be the likeness of a Dun Laoghaire housewife who in the 1940s had (obviously with some abandon and allegedly for charitable purposes) entered a fancy-dress competition. 'It just seemed to have the right feel!', explained the Irish archaeologist who sent it.

By now, as if using a type of instinctive litmus paper, I was becoming adept at sorting out these false trails from the true leads. When a woman in Suffolk wrote to tell me that following the early death of her husband's uncle, a surveyor called Ignatius Dracopoli, his widow Isolde had married Beaumont-Thomas, I knew at once that this 'Isolde' must actually be the peripatetic 'Iseult', and felt for a moment I was on the verge of catching her up. I suspected that Iseult Beaumont-Thomas was probably the wife of Reggie's elder brother Lionel. At this point another member of the Beaumont-Thomas family (actually a rare Treherne-Thomas) wrote to introduce himself, claiming that 'as both your grandfather and my father's first cousin Reggie Beaumont-Thomas enjoyed Agnes May's favours – at least she was married to Reggie! – we seem to have a tenuous connection'.

The Beaumont-Thomases (including their several mutations into Treherne-Thomases, Spence-Thomases, Massey-Thomases, Wyndham-Thomases, etc.) were, he reminded me, a very wealthy family. Their great fortune had been created through the steel industry in Wales during the nineteenth century, initially by the son of a Somerset coal merchant and then enlarged by his son and two grandsons, the elder of whom was Reggie's and Lionel's father. My correspondent sent me some pages photocopied from a privately printed history of these variously prefaced Thomases, *Men of Steel* by David Wainwright (Quiller Press, 1986). I had never heard of this book and read the enclosed pages with interest.

There was only one mention of Agnes May's Reginald Beaumont-Thomas – simply recording his birth as Lionel's younger brother. In commercial terms Reggie was obviously a man of no importance. But I was able to learn much about this family so curiously entwined with my own. His brother's life appeared to occupy a whole chapter.

Lionel had been born in 1893, was educated at Rugby, and later served in Belgium and France during the war. He had been married twice – to the same woman: the daughter of an officer in the Colonial Service. The first time, in June 1913, they had married in secret at the Paddington Register Office, Lionel (as I later discovered) adding a year to his age to make him a full twenty-one, the same age as his wife. The reason for this secrecy was the violent opposition from Lionel's mother, Nora, who disapproved of love matches, having herself married for reasons of pure wealth and position. She was extremely ambitious on behalf of her elder son and wanted him to make an advantageous marriage, perhaps into the aristocracy. To separate him from his girlfriend, she arranged for him to be sent to Luxembourg for a year, ostensibly on steel-making business – a move which actually precipitated their marrying in secret. When Lionel returned, in the summer of 1914, still in love with the same girl, his mother at last gave her grudging consent to their union – only to be told that they were already man and wife. This prompted a monumental rift in the family that was finally settled by the First World War, at the beginning of which, on Nora's insistence, a second wedding ceremony, this one at Holy Trinity, Brompton, was performed.

Lionel was to take part in almost all the major military engagements of the war along the Western Front. At the beginning of 1917, he was awarded the Military Cross. But his father Richard, attending the investiture at Buckingham Palace to see King George V confer this decoration on his son, caught a chill that led, a fortnight later, to his death at the age of fifty-six. Lionel then became a director of the steelworks while still a serving officer. There is no mention of Reginald because he was ten years younger than his brother and still at school – suddenly a very wealthy fifteen-year-old.

In any case, all their mother's ambitions seem to have been channelled through the active brother, Lionel. In the early 1920s he stood as a Conservative candidate in two safe Welsh Labour seats and on one occasion, his car being trapped by angry miners, he escaped on foot across the hills. Impressed by his resolution and speed, the Conservative Party adopted him for the more promising King's Norton division of Birmingham which he narrowly won in 1929 against the national swing to Labour. 'I have had to write so many letters of condolence to-day, that it is a real pleasure to be able to congratulate you on your magnificent win,' the Prime Minister, Neville Chamberlain, wrote to him. He won the seat again in 1931, was given a junior post in Ramsay MacDonald's National Government, and tipped for a powerful political future. Then suddenly, in the spring of

1933, he announced his resignation 'owing to ill-health'. This somewhat baffled me. Neville Chamberlain's letter, reluctantly accepting his resignation, seemed to hint at other reasons, hidden reasons, for abandoning such a short-lived and promising political life.

I am naturally very grieved to hear that you feel you cannot continue to remain a member; and while I fully realise your difficulties and appreciate that it is only the exigencies of the situation which have led to such a decision, I shall always be very sorry that you have had to cut short your political career.

Such language did not seem quite appropriate for serious illness. Besides, Lionel was healthy enough to be accepted for renewed army service six years later, and in 1942 was appointed head of a British Military Mission which set off for the Middle East.

On the last photocopied page, I learnt a little more about him. The life of a Member of Parliament, David Wainwright ominously wrote

is time-consuming and a heavy strain on personal relationships . . . Social life is liable to be disrupted, and the effect on family life can be devastating. Lionel Beaumont-Thomas was approaching 40, tall (he was six foot five inches), balding but fair-haired and fair-complexioned, with a 'good war record', and wealthy. When in London, he lived on his yacht moored on the

Thames opposite the Houses of Parliament, to which he was ferried by launch. It was an impressive setting even for a period when rich men would be admired for demonstrating their wealth in outward show. Devoted to his wife and family, he nevertheless had an eye for pretty women.

What this seemed to tell me was that I had been wrong in assuming the mysterious Iseult to have been Lionel's wife. In the account of his career I was reading, she was named as Pauline, and her maiden name was not Dracopoli but Marriott. As for his brother, 'I do not think Reggie had any children, and I doubt that he ever married again,' my correspondent ended his letter. 'He was always going on sea voyages and breaking his legs.' The copyright line in *Men of Steel,* he pointed out, named Pearl Brewis along with David Wainwright. 'The person you really need is Mrs Pearl Brewis – Reggie was her uncle.'

News of my book must have been travelling among the family, though they were not, I later discovered, normally fond of communicating with one another. A few days later I was opening a letter from Pearl Brewis, Lionel and Pauline Beaumont-Thomas's daughter. She had been reading *Basil Street Blues* and had found the chapter about my Aunt Yolande and her relationship with Hazlehurst particularly interesting. She had immediately recognised the photograph of Hazlehurst. In the early 1930s his yacht *Frothblower* used to be moored next to her father's yacht *Pauline* in Cubitt's Yacht Basin at Chiswick (when it was not stationed opposite

the Houses of Parliament), and it was on *Frothblower* that
Lionel had met Iseult – and her two children. But the
photograph I had reproduced came from the late 1930s on
board a yacht called *Llanthony*, which I had also
mentioned in my book (Hazel wrote a series of love letters to
Yolande from it).

'My father had extreme money worries during the early
'thirties, & was very vulnerable at that time to be attracted
by Iseult who, as my mother used to say, "set her cap at
him",' Pearl Brewis wrote.

> He insisted on leaving my mother to marry Iseult &
> made the necessary arrangements by paying someone to
> spend the night with him. This ended his parliamentary
> career, and he had to excuse himself on grounds of 'ill
> health'. My father sold the yacht 'Pauline', named after
> my mother, & bought the 'Llanthony' . . .
>
> I have several albums of photographs showing
> yachting in the canals & the South of France, but am
> unable to identify many of the people. These date from
> 1930–1940. Maybe your aunt and Hazel are among
> them. Hazel and my father certainly remained friends.

Having read this, I did something obvious which I should
have done very much earlier: I looked up Lionel Beaumont-
Thomas in *Who Was Who*. I had been unable to find his
death certificate, but nevertheless saw his name listed in the
1941–50 volume, where it is noted that he died in December
1942. Diplomatically, no date is recorded for his marriage to

Pauline Marriott, and therefore no confusion is created round their two weddings. But a date is given for the dissolution of their marriage. It is 1934, the year he later married his second wife. Her name is Iseult Hazlehurst.

But who *was* Iseult Hazlehurst? I still hadn't pinned her down. Probably, I thought, she was Hazel's sister. That would fit the facts in so far as I knew them, and explain how Lionel Beaumont-Thomas had met her on his yacht and became a friend of her brother. Having two children meant, of course, that she had probably been married and then, after the death of, or divorce from, her husband, reverted to her maiden name as many women did and do. Certainly she could not be either of the two women in my article, Agnes May or Yolande.

I had enough new evidence now to do more checking of births, deaths and marriages. I also planned to visit Pearl Brewis in Hampshire, and made arrangements to meet Carmen's family friend who had known Hazlehurst and now lived in Chelsea. But first I read again carefully through Hazel's love letters to my Aunt Yolande.

There are several references to 'the family', but all of them turn out to mean the Holroyd family – there are no other Hazlehursts mentioned in any of the letters. These surviving letters begin in the early summer of 1933, that is not long after Yolande's father Fraser, my grandfather, returned from his six-year fling with Agnes May. Already Hazel and Yolande seem very close, and have discussed, even argued about, their previous relationships. 'I know why I failed before, and yet I refuse to learn,' Hazel writes by way of apology after one of these arguments. 'In both cases I was so damned inferior to them, and they naturally couldn't stick it, & moved on. Bobs so aptly expressed it one day – "The Starling after the Eagle" – & it quite confirmed my own private opinion. Now what's the answer to *you*. You are so very much superior to both before, then I must of necessity be found that amount worse off.'

This is unusual: a man claiming so much convoluted 'inferiority' to his previous girlfriends as well as to his present love. Perhaps he is genuinely distrustful of himself, or else simply using this device to defuse more damaging emotional arguments from Yolande. She, though obviously in love, is cautious, and slightly suspicious of Hazel, who reassures her: 'As for naughtiness & wickedness, no. There has been no temptation, & if there was, I would be quite sufficiently unmoved . . . I never missed anyone so much & never felt so completely dependent upon one person before. All feelings I had for Bobs were water compared with what I feel for you. I never hope to be fonder of anyone, for it really hurts, & I'm afraid, so very afraid . . . All my love my one own darling Yolande. H.'

There is a further mention of Yolande's predecessor, the curiously named Bobs, in another letter that year, also written from the yacht *Frothblower*. 'I had a letter from Bobs,' he writes, 'and she said she hopes Yolande is sweet to me for I am a very dear person in some ways & she is so glad I am completely cured of her. She is so happy.'

Otherwise, though there are descriptions of yachting trips,

there is no identification of the other people who are on board. He mentions that he is starting a new business and asks permission to make Yolande his nominee on the board of the company – a preliminary, he hopes, to their names being joined, once this business is successful, in marriage.

I can make better sense of my aunt's caution and Hazel's self-deprecation once I have spoken to someone who knew him. Myfi Heim, whose name Carmen has given me, appears immediately to solve one of my intractable problems: why I had been unable to find any record of Hazlehurst's birth. 'He told me he was born in Ireland (his mother's name was Nelly) and that both his parents had been killed in a car accident there,' she says. Hazlehurst himself, apparently, was very keen on racing cars. She approves of this, being herself an outdoor woman who hunts, fishes, and is a crack shot. To ease our conversation indoors, she pours us each a hefty glass of champagne.

I tell her of my Aunt Yolande's long attachment to him, and how devastated she had been to hear of his sudden marriage in Italy during the Second World War. Myfi Heim knew about this.

'He was stationed in Salerno,' she tells me, 'and commandeered an apartment belonging to an Italian lady who lived in the house with her two daughters. He married the elder daughter, Palmina Abbagnano, who was nineteen, and brought her back to Cheshire where he had been posted at the beginning of the war – several ladies there were very disappointed to see him return with a wife (he always, by the way, called her "Prunella"). Everybody loved his company –

he was lively, quick-witted, good fun. He owned a tough little naval schooner then, called *Black Pearl*.'

'What was his business?'

'He was a consultant engineer – and very good with boats. He would take everyone out on *Black Pearl* – dogs and children too.'

'Did he have any children of his own?'

'No, he didn't. His marriage to "Prunella" didn't last very long. They were divorced quite soon after the war.'

'Did you ever hear him speak of my Aunt Yolande?'

'No. Never. He used to speak of Bobs or Bobby rather bitterly sometimes. She was an earlier wife.'

'He was married to Bobs?'

'Yes, I think so. He told me he was married at seventeen, but quarrelled with his wife over a game of croquet on their honeymoon, and never saw her again.'

'I'm astonished.'

'He was full of stories like that.'

'Did he have a sister?'

'Not that I heard of. I can't remember a sister.'

'Someone called Iseult?'

'I think that was his wife, Bobby. He was always giving people new names.'

Each new name I heard added to my confusion, as if I were playing a complicated game – the Parting of Names – the rules of which, as in a worrying dream, hadn't yet been explained to me. Hazlehurst had no first name as yet, but the women had so many: Agnes May, Vera, Bobs, Iseult, Isolde, Nelly, Nora, Yolande, Pauline, Palmina, Prunella, Pearl – my head was spinning with them. We had, I discovered, finished the bottle of champagne. And I was coming away with one extra name, that of Palmina's younger sister. Her name was Mariolina.

Mariolina, who lives in Chelsea, remembers Hazel very well. For a brief time, she had been his sister-in-law. 'He used to drive sports cars, and spoke quite a bit of his hunting days. He'd also won a wonderful lot of silver cups in yachting races. Altogether he was a very dashing figure, amusing, highly attractive and of course athletic – also very good with children. My daughter Tessa worshipped him, though I remember him telling her off for eating too much, and scolding her severely for reading *Lady Chatterley's Lover*. He could be rather strict – especially with anyone who was sick on his boat when he took them out to sea. Occasionally, too, he could be quite snobbish. He objected strongly to my son being sent to Harrow. He himself, as you know, had gone to Eton – though he admitted to having run away! Incidentally, he was decorated by the King at Buckingham Palace. But you can see all that in his *Who's Who* entry.'

'He was in *Who's Who*?'

'Definitely. I remember him telling me so.'

I feel doubly stupid, having also failed to look up Lionel Beaumont-Thomas in *Who's Who*. But later, when I hunt through the volumes of *Who Was Who*, I cannot see his name; and when I write to the archivist at Eton College Library, she cannot find him in the Register of Old Etonians. 'In my experience boys said to have run away from Eton were rarely here in the first place,' she wrote, 'so I am not altogether surprised.'

I had one more person to visit, Pearl Brewis, who united in my mind the Hazlehurst, Holroyd and Beaumont-Thomas stories, being Lionel and Pauline Beaumont-Thomas's daughter, a one-time stepdaughter of Iseult, and niece of Reggie Beaumont-Thomas. Surely she would be able to bring clarity to this dense plot.

By one of those coincidences that mean nothing and lead nowhere, but suggest the interconnectedness of all life, I saw with surprise that Pearl Brewis lived only a mile or so away from Myrtle Cottage, on the edge of the New Forest, near Brockenhurst, where Agnes May's mother, Robina Bickerstaff, died in the summer of 1943. Pearl knew nothing of Agnes May's mother, but she did meet Agnes May herself shortly before the war. This was the first person I had met who had seen my grandfather's inamorata. I felt I was taking one step closer to her.

In *Basil Street Blues* I was unable to take this story beyond 1936 when, Agnes May's second husband, Thomas Babb, having divorced her (citing my grandfather as co-respondent), she immediately married Reggie Beaumont-Thomas. For a couple of years they had lived together in Kensington – then they left London and I lost track of them. Pearl Brewis can tell me where they went and what then happened.

They went to a small town in Hertfordshire called Bushey where Reggie bought a house on the heath called The Tubs. It was not far from Pinewood Film Studios at Elstree. He and Agnes May would often invite actors and actresses over for parties – there seemed to be parties going on all the time. The large garden with its splendid swimming pool was perfect for summer gatherings, and at night they would play in one of the rooms on the ground floor that had been made into a private casino or 'gambling den'. One way and another, the house was like a miniature Hollywood. Agnes May herself, with her brass-blonde hair, was known as 'the American barmaid'. People called her 'Maimie' which amused her.

I felt a jolt of recognition on hearing this, and noticed later that on her first marriage certificate (when marrying William Lisle at the age of twenty in 1916) she had given her first name as 'Maimie Archie'.

Pearl Brewis had met Agnes May only once. But among the pile of correspondence, photos and albums she had gathered together for me to examine was a letter written by her father Lionel on 30 October 1942. 'Just seen Reggie,' he writes. 'He is very well and looking a lot better, having got rid of his wife. He has bought a bungalow down near Brighton.'

Though they never got a divorce, Agnes May and Reggie seem to have separated permanently. He made her an allowance (rather as my grandfather had done): it was rumoured to have been a lump sum of several thousand pounds plus an annuity of almost two thousand pounds (tax-free) a year – similar to a financial arrangement he had made ten years before, following the divorce from his French wife, Germaine Blanche Aimée Dubor. He then went to live with Vera, the ex-wife of a dentist, who took the name Thomas and lived with him near Brighton until his death nearly thirty years later.

Pearl did not know what became of Agnes May after 1942, so I asked her some questions about her Uncle Reggie.

'He was immensely tall,' she tells me, 'almost seven feet (Lionel himself was a good six foot five inches). He had a small head and was semi-paralysed on one side (either it was infantile paralysis or else "sleepy sickness"). Decidedly he was very far from romantic to look at. Yet he was a playboy and exercised a passion for fast cars – "one foot on the accelerator, one foot in the grave" was his motto. Unlike Lionel, he never worked, never had a job – except for a brief period when he acted for Rolls-Royce as consultant on their coachwork. He loved cars. He once owned five Packards.'

I then ask her about her father, Lionel Beaumont-Thomas.

'It was a terrible shock when he fell in love with Iseult Hazlehurst and divorced my mother – I don't think she ever got over it, and it ruined his career too. Iseult already had two sons, Nick and Jack, but she and Lionel did not have any children of their own – which was just as well as Lionel and Pauline had four. This wasn't an easy time for me and my brothers – Richard suffered from a chronic illness and was permanently in hospital from the age of sixteen, and Nigel had asthma.'

'But who was Iseult?'

'Her two sons have the surname Dracopoli – that was their father's name . . .'

'So she wasn't married to Hazlehurst?'

'I thought she was.'

'Another marriage?'

'Must be.'

For Pearl Brewis, this is looking back into 'another lifetime'. She had been born in 1921, the youngest of Lionel and Pauline's children. She was twelve when they divorced, and twenty when she married in 1940. As a trainee nurse, she had sailed with her husband to Burma where she joined the Women's Auxiliary Service. Bombed and machine-gunned, she somehow managed to keep up a canteen service for troops in the front line, as well as nursing the wounded soldiers in searing heat at primitive military hospitals. She was like the heroine of a fast-paced, adventure-packed novel by Nevil Shute. She was to give birth to a son in the mission hospital at Shillong following an earthquake – with its awful trembling and roaring, and the tremendous chasms opening in the ground, this was more frightening than anything she had experienced in the fighting zones, retreating just ahead of the Japanese during the Burma campaign. Shortly after the birth news came that her husband was dead. Her brother Nigel too, with whom she was very close, was later killed in action. Her father also died. The reason why I could never find his death certificate was that his body had been lost at sea when the ship on which he was sailing on a secret mission concerning the Allied landings on Crete was torpedoed in the Caribbean at the end of 1942. But Pearl and her son came through the war.

Pearl is a fighter, a survivor. She has a good, strong face, with a firm chin, beaked nose, wide forehead. There is something Churchillian about her. She is almost eighty and suffering from osteoporosis and arthritis. She is unable to stand without acute pain, but she is tough and independent-minded, full of life, and has devised a number of ingenious ways of getting around. She uses two sticks, as she advances, her cat Tiddles playing around them. We gossip: and she hands me a pile of legal papers concerning her family which looks very like the legal papers that piled up round my own family, and so many families. 'It is a disaster,' she says, pointing at these papers, and she laughs.

Once she was Pearl Beaumont-Thomas, and what she tells me helps to identify the regiment of Mrs Beaumont-Thomases I have amassed. I knew now that Nora Beaumont-Thomas had married into the steel business and became the ambitious mother of Lionel, and the mother of Reggie too. I knew that Germaine Blanche Aimée Beaumont-Thomas was Reggie's first wife (a Parisian dancing girl, according to Pearl) whom he left in France, before marrying Agnes May. I also knew that Pauline Beaumont-Thomas (Pearl's mother) was Lionel's first wife, and that Iseult Beaumont-Thomas, Lionel's second wife, was, as his widow, to evolve into the robust and unforgettable Mrs B-T of Highgate Village, before energetically retiring to East Anglia. Finally I knew that Vera Beaumont-Thomas was that slim and stylish lady (ex-wife of a dentist) who, when Agnes May Beaumont-Thomas left Reggie to pursue her further adventures, nursed him in his wheelchair through his many affluent last years in Brighton.

So, having seen my way through these ranks of Mrs Beaumont-Thomases, I emerged at last. But had I gathered enough clues to fashion a story, actually two interconnected stories, from such random and confusing facts, such rumours of fact? Could I use these bits and pieces as sources of light, strange stars, by which to plot a clear and explanatory narrative? This was what I must try to do. I would begin with my Aunt Yolande's fiancé, the elusive Hazlehurst.

His name was not Hazlehurst. When he corrected my aunt with such decisive capital letters, he was in fact misleading her. The change was not great, but it was enough to fool me later when hunting for his birth. Henry Edward Haselhurst was born, not in Ireland, but in the small town of Beverley, in north-east Yorkshire, on 12 March 1894, the elder son of Louis Haselhurst, a journeyman in a chemical manure works there, and his wife, Maria Annie (née Appleton). She was the eldest daughter of a local grocer who had died shortly before her marriage in 1890. She had been working as a hosier's assistant at the Wednesday market (her mother was a draper) and seems to have continued working until the birth of her son. But why had she not given birth earlier in her marriage? It was most unusual. Had Henry perhaps been adopted? Not officially, of course, but privately as sometimes happened in those days. Only very few people would know the facts, especially if some grand family were involved in the transaction. In the north of England, secrecy was highly prized over such matters. And if this were true, then it would account for the sense of difference, the feeling of not belonging, that grew in the boy's imagination.

His mother, Maria Annie, being two years older than her husband, was aged thirty-three when Henry Edward was born and thirty-five at the birth of her second son, Roland Percy. He was rather a dull boy and really did seem to be an authentic child of this journeyman and hosier's assistant. But perhaps Henry had been billeted on them with an allowance which enabled them to afford a child of their own – someone not given the names of English kings as he had been given. These were the sort of speculations that could burden or enrich your life – burden it at home and enrich it whenever you escaped from home.

There were many Appletons in and around Beverley at that time, and even more Haselhursts. Louis Haselhurst seems to have been a steady enough chap. He was the third of nine children, his father William being classed as 'a labourer', sometimes described as a fireman, but more probably a foreman, at the Tigar Manure Company in Beverley. The company works stood in Grovehill Road where the Haselhurst family lived. It had been founded in 1825 by a chemist and grocer called Pennock Tigar, originally making paint, and then adding fertilisers which became its main product. Louis's two elder brothers became a commercial traveller and a clerk for a leather merchant in Beverley, his younger brother was to be the local millwright, and two of his sisters elementary school teachers there. Louis himself left school at fourteen and followed his father into the Tigar manure works, initially as a general labourer, finally as a chemist. He remained there all his working life – that is until 1923 when the manure works closed and he, at the age of sixty, retired. His was the most regular of lives. But there was one irregularity: his birth was not recorded. He was a man apparently without a birth certificate. Because, I finally discovered, his name had been entered in the index as Haselchurch. Damn and blast!

On their marriage Louis and his wife went to live in a small house, 6 Rose Villas, in Wilbert Lane, less than a quarter of a mile west of Grovehill Road. In 1904, with their two sons, they moved again, this time a quarter of a mile south, to a rather larger house, 24 Flemingate, next to the railway line. There was room for a domestic servant, Priscella Hart, in her young teens. Henry was then aged ten and his brother Roland eight.

It was not very long after this that something unusual happened. All the Haselhurst family had been educated and employed in Beverley, but Henry was sent, not as he claimed to Eton, but to the Hull Municipal Technical College which offered an excellent five-year course in engineering. The class records have been destroyed but Henry must have successfully completed the course since he was to earn his living as a qualified mechanical and electrical engineer, and as a 'fuel technologist'. The entry age at Hull was eleven, so Henry would have gone there in 1905 and left in 1910 when, instead of returning to Beverley, he went off to join the Royal Engineers as a private soldier and was sent to Singapore. On the army records he has left blank the name of his father and mother.

Something terrible must have happened. From the age of sixteen he was never again to see his parents or his younger brother. None of them would be present at any of his weddings, and he did not go to his brother's wedding in Beverley. His mother was to die at the age of eighty in 1941. Roland is present at her death, but Henry, who is then writing letters to my Aunt Yolande, does not mention his mother dying. Neither in her will, nor later in that of her husband, is there any mention of him. When Louis Haselhurst dies the following year he is described in the *Beverley Guardian* as 'beloved husband of the late Annie and dear dad of Roland (Jim) and [daughter-]in-law Cissie'. There is no acknowledgement of his having had another son, his elder son Henry. The break is absolute on both sides for over thirty years – and then another thirty years, since the two brothers do not acknowledge each other's existence even at their deaths in the 1970s. Only on his marriage certificate is Henry obliged to own up to having a father named Louis (though he sometimes misspells the name and always gives this long-term journeyman and chemical labourer at the manure works the superior-sounding rank of 'Gentleman', which, after Louis's death, at Henry's last marriage of all, he improves with the additional words 'of independent means').

This retrospective improvement is nicely in keeping with Henry's own successful career. He was to find another way of life in the army, a life of travel and adventure, and through this activity, stretching over a dozen years, part of it abroad, he also found a new identity.

He had a good war, a very good war. At the start, having come back from Singapore, he was appointed to a commission in the King's (Liverpool) Regiment. Then, in the spring of 1915, he was posted to France with the First Battalion and promoted to a full lieutenant. He would have met no one from Beverley in his regiment, or in the Royal Welch Fusiliers to which he was later attached. The young men of Beverley were being invited to join the East Yorkshire

Regiment, which Roland Haselhurst, still only twenty, obediently did with a friend in August 1915 – two months before the Derby Scheme to encourage recruitment was introduced. Unlike his brother he was never commissioned, though he did 'see action' in Egypt, this theatre of war being the only foreign country to which he travelled all his life. At the end of the war, he left the army, still a private soldier, and returned to his parents' house in Beverley where he lived until his death over fifty years later.

How different from Henry! On some of the forms he was obliged to fill in during his life, he would put, in place of his birth, the date of his baptism (at St John's Minster, when he was five weeks old, on 14 April 1894), as if he were a child of God. This illusion was enhanced when, early in 1916, he was transferred to the Royal Flying Corps.

The Royal Flying Corps had grown from the balloon companies of the Royal Engineers which operated air observation in the Sudan and during the Boer War. By the beginning of the First World War, though it had an establishment of officers seconded from the regular army, and men from the Royal Engineers, very few of its kites and amphibians, its biplanes, airships, its great dirigibles and magical lighter-than-air machines were fit for use in war. This was partly because, though some young visionaries already saw 'men moving swiftly through the air on simple surfaces for military purposes', officials at the War Office, senior commanders, convinced that these so-called 'aeroplanes' were sheer essays in lunacy, had made almost no money available for experimentation and development.

Pilots in those early days of the war were often buccaneers, frightened of nothing except perhaps the danger of this war ending too soon (before they really got a chance to enjoy it). They were fuelled by romance, guided by a love of display, artists in aviation who, rather than rely on some scholar's finicky map, would put down, even make forced landings, to enquire of astonished pedestrians their way to a target. Their main function once they got there was to shoot film and take back their photographs of enemy movements. Occasionally, by way of encouragement, they might lob a grenade or two over the side, but when they passed German planes on their way to reconnoitre allied lines, they would hail one another with comradely salutes. It was splendid sport, and these pilots developed very affectionate relationships with their planes, naming them after their mothers or girlfriends, Susannah, Jo, Merrill, Valerie, Linda, Janet and so on. Of course it was a dangerous game they were playing, they all knew that. There were crashes and splashes and the most terrific exploits when wounded chaps flying upside down, literally hanging out of their machines, guiding the controls with their feet like marvellous performers in a circus, would somehow get themselves back to the aircraft park, dead or alive. Most exciting of all were the solo missions to land secret agents, with their flocks of pigeons (each one a trained messenger bird) far into enemy territory, leaving themselves just enough fuel to make it home.

By the time Haselhurst joined, these buccaneering days of the lone, valiant pilot, great knights of the air, had passed, though their legendary deeds still lingered in everyone's memory and imagination. The Royal Flying Corps was now a well-knit, professional group of expert aviators. At the School of Instruction, over four months, Haselhurst was taught the arts of formation flying and night flying, how to fire the new Lewis guns attached to the wings when intervening in battles on the surface, how to win freedom of movement in the air (while denying it to enemy aircraft), and how to take photos from every possible angle – even when travelling as fast as seventy or eighty miles an hour! He learnt wireless telegraphy, bombing and the dropping of propaganda leaflets, and by the second week of June 1916 he was finally made a flying officer and wore a bright new uniform.

That summer, in France, began the greatest continuous battle the world had seen: the Battle of the Somme. In later years, Haselhurst would sometimes speak of it to his stepsons, telling them how it began over rolling uplands dotted with little patches of wood, the long corridor of kites looking down in ominous silence from both sides on this vast stage of war, while hundreds of aeroplanes, buzzing like wasps, patrolled the long lines of trenches showing up starkly in the chalky earth. Then the bombardment opened, and they dodged in between the rockets and phosphorus shells, searching for the red flares of their troops. Sometimes thick clouds hung over the country, and the mist and sleet were so impenetrable that they had to fly almost into the trenches themselves, and were flung around like corks in the barrage. But they brought back amazing pictures of the ground fighting: the spouting of the earth under the bombardment (with the terrible noise of exploding shells); the thin lines of men moving erratically forward; the streams of distress flares; then the counter-barrage growing into an awful wall of fire, and the grey figures coming up from their battered dug-outs, as if resurrected from the dead only to be killed again. It seemed never-ending.

You could see too, from your seat in the sky, a new secret weapon belonging to the allies: the tank. It appeared rather a ludicrous toy as it ambled down village streets, falling into trenches and even apparently attempting to climb trees: comic stuff in the magnificent spectacle.

This was a new type of warfare, and the planes flew increasingly, without rest, as if in a dream. Though there were vivid air battles, the vast cost of blood was to be spent on the ground, and the pilots were grateful to be away from those grim infantry encounters, tense, almost motionless tugs-of-war to and fro, which they witnessed below.

For Haselhurst himself, it appears, this flying held a peculiar appeal. To escape from the solid world of fact and rise into another element, a more fantastical element, was like an evolutionary ascent, a metamorphosis. The old life at Beverley, which had clung to him so damply, was left far behind as if it never belonged to him. He had shed it like the skin of a caterpillar, a chrysalis that becomes a butterfly. He was out, out of that narrow house in Flemingate by the railway line, and could go where he liked, be what he wanted. A blue sunny sky stretched before him. He was free.

There is no record of where Haselhurst flew or what he actually did over the period of the war beyond what he afterwards told people. It is clear that he was still a lieutenant at the end of the war, and that he had been given the three medals all such surviving soldiers received: the 1914 Star, the British War Medal and the Victory Medal. Sometimes, in later years, he wore a patch over one eye, and this, he let it be known, was on account of a war wound. Was he blind in one eye?* Sometimes, literally, he was – or so he said; at other times, metaphorically perhaps, though this may have been more of a wink at the world. Then, occasionally, the patch would give way to a monocle, but that was more for evening wear.

Against so much that was blurred, a few, rock-like facts stand out. Early in 1918 he is serving as an equipment officer (3rd Class) at a School of Aeronautics, and a little later he was transferred to a junior post at the Air Ministry, formed that year shortly before the Royal Flying Corps was re-organised into the Royal Air Force. All officers were given the option of transferring to the new force or retaining their army commission. After a short delay, Haselhurst chose to rejoin the King's (Liverpool) Regiment. There were, perhaps, two reasons for his choice. Though flying was endless fun, there would probably be less time in the air for him now that he was entering his late twenties – this air cavalry was for the very young. And then, the Royal Air Force did not have the social calibre and career prospects of

---

*His name does not appear in *The Sky Their Battlefield*, the massive list of those wounded in the air during the First World War compiled by Trevor Henshaw (Grub Street, 1995).

the army. And this was all the more important now because, on 11 September 1918, two months before the armistice, he married.

Cicely Last, his bride, was nineteen, the daughter of an Indian civil servant who had recently died. They were married in Bath. Her mother and sister were at the wedding, but of course none of his family. The story he later told of their parting following a quarrelsome game of croquet on their honeymoon seems far-fetched since his wife did not actually start divorce proceedings for another six years. It is easy to see how this wartime pilot from the skies might have appeared to her like a splendid eagle. But those days were soon over. Early in the summer of 1920 he was posted with his regiment to Ireland. Here, in these violent times, he concocted his parents' deaths in a car accident. He loved speed and had taken to racing cars himself, which may have given him the idea. He also claimed, from time to time, that he had been born in Ireland. Something did die there and something else was born. At the beginning of June 1922 he retired from the army with the rank of captain, and came back to England – but not to his wife Cicely who petitioned for a divorce on the grounds of his desertion. She was impatient to start again, having fallen in love with another man, Alec Carrie. He was the very opposite of a high flyer: a submarine man, naval officer, whom she married soon after the divorce came through. The following year, he gave her what she wanted – what Haselhurst had never given her: a son, whom they christened Michael. It is sometimes difficult to understand earlier parts of our lives. Of course, she was very vulnerable so soon after her father's death. But looking back, Cicely's one-time eagle appeared little more than a sparrow. 'Husband number two was the hero,' remembers her nephew, who grew up believing Haselhurst to have been 'a great, even shameful mistake, a charmer but a bounder; a cad even. So no photos exist, as far as I know, not even a wedding photo . . .'

But for others Haselhurst was still a romantic figure. Popularly known as 'Captain Haselhurst', he set himself up as a consultant engineer – a 'senior partner' as he sometimes described it, though he appeared to be working rather cleverly for himself and he was often away in Europe. He loved travelling, leaving places and people, as he loved speeding, loved flying, racing, moving on. He kept a little biplane at Brooklands where he also kept his car. It was a mystery how he could afford such expensive toys. No one remembers how he caught up with the mysterious Iseult, or more probably she caught up with him. There was no escaping Iseult once she had you in her sights – everyone agreed on that.

Iseult's father, Oscar Bland, came from a wealthy shipping family in Ireland, and lived rather grandly with his wife at Ettington in Warwickshire. In the summer of 1914, on the very day Britain declared war on Germany, Iseult had married a man with the exotic name of Ignatius Dracopoli. He was a twenty-six-year-old, up-and-coming surveyor from Chalfont St Giles. She was nineteen and still living with her parents. But she had a mind of her own. She was eager to shed her inappropriate maiden name and get on with life.

Bland she was not. No threat of a world war, nor even the eruption of war itself, was to disturb her plans. Both families were summoned to the smart wedding at Stratford, and over the next eight years Iseult had two sons, Nick and then Jack whose birth coincided with his father's early death from cancer in 1923. He had left his widow with precious little money – six or seven thousand pounds. It would not take her very long to get through that with two children to educate. What made things worse was that her father's wealth had suddenly dried up. One day while he and his wife were in Paris they found that they did not have enough money to get home. The Bland family came to the rescue, paid off his debts and shipped him off to Rhodesia where they set him up as a farmer. But when Iseult and her mother went out to visit him, they found old Bland in a bar, drunk and destitute again. He liked the country life, he explained, and was recognised everywhere as an excellent shot: unfortunately he excelled at nothing else – certainly not farming. So he was shipped back to England. But from now on he was to be nothing but a financial liability.

Iseult needed a man with money to entertain her and help with the education of her children. Captain Haselhurst appeared to be that man. He had a small but apparently prosperous engineering business of his own – and his aeroplanes, his racing car and the yacht he was talking of buying reassured her: they were the playthings surely of a rich man. He was full of charm too, got on well with her father (both fancied themselves as good shots), and liked her two boys, though he did not appear to want children of his own, which was just as well. He was a couple of years older than she was and had briefly come to rest at Hoop Cottage, a few yards down Green Lane in Little Haddam where she was temporarily living after her husband's death. She decided to marry him.

Now aged thirty, Iseult was still a good-looking woman, fair-haired, always smartly dressed and with expensive tastes. She was also an excellent cook (and much enjoyed complaining about the food in fashionable restaurants). Haselhurst was dazzled by her, caught in the headlights. It was she who made the decision to marry – she made most of the decisions. As one of her sons later observed, she could give anyone a good run for his money and never took no for an answer. So, on 12 June 1926, she married Haselhurst.

This was very good news for the boys. Before long, their new stepfather, the Captain, was taking them both to Brooklands. Jack, the younger, was fearfully sick at first in his biplane, but eventually got used to it; and Nick enjoyed whizzing round the track in his racing car. Haselhurst would tell the boys all about the amazing races he had won and his exploits in the war. He showed them his medals too. It was as if he were a boy himself.

In 1929, he joined the British Motor Boat Company, and during the early Thirties, having given up flying, would often sail along the English and northern French coasts on his yacht *Frothblower*. This was the period when my Aunt Yolande got to know him (the 'H' with which he signed his letters stood for Henry, not Hazlehurst as I had imagined). He also bought a fifteen-ton motor cruiser named

Mongoose. Sometimes he would go off exploring the waterways of Holland, France and Belgium, and once or twice went as far south as the Mediterranean with another boat enthusiast who was moored next to him in Cubitt's Yacht Basin at Chiswick. This was the Member of Parliament Lionel Beaumont-Thomas.

My family spent several weekends on Haselhurst's yachts in the 1930s, particularly on *Llanthony* which he later borrowed from Lionel Beaumont-Thomas. Inevitably they must have come across Lionel at one time or another, and perhaps even caught sight of his enormously tall brother Reggie – the two brothers were on friendly terms and quite frequently saw each other. But the Holroyds (my father, my aunt and even my grandfather) had only walk-on parts in the unfolding drama of these boats.

It was soon apparent that the Haselhurst marriage was not turning out well. Though Iseult had been taken with her new husband at first, she soon found him to be a man of straw. He had far less money than she supposed – at any rate, he did after three or four years of marriage to her. The more she got to know him, the less substantial and manly he appeared to be. The eagle had soared: a sparrow landed. Behind all his role-playing, he was never really a confident self-possessed man – what self was there to possess? She could not make anything much of him. She knew that his claims to have won all sorts of races were false – made up probably to impress the boys, but it didn't impress her. Eventually she put him down as an amiable rogue. But like her father, she discovered, he drank. Why did men she knew take to drink? What could it be? Henry, she thought, drank to be rid of himself, perhaps to be rid of her. In which case, she decided, he must have his way. Much as he liked the look of women, he was essentially a man's man, or more precisely a child's man, happiest perhaps in the army, but drifting nowhere in particular through civilian life in his cars and boats. It was time for her to disembark . . .

. . . and to embark perhaps on the next boat. Lionel's wife, Pauline Beaumont-Thomas, soon began to have qualms about this neighbour of theirs in Cubitt's Yacht Basin. She used to hear her sometimes calling out to her husband Lionel from *Frothblower*. 'Leo! Leo!' she would call. It made her feel curiously uneasy – though in fact it was ridiculous: no one called him Leo. He was Lionel.

Pauline was only four or five years older than Iseult, but she appeared more mature. She had classical good looks but never troubled to dress smartly. Good breeding rather than good clothes – that was her. She was a country woman who liked walking and riding: those sorts of things. Usually in Herefordshire. At Great Bampton. Mind you, she was a damned handsome woman. According to her friends she resembled Elizabeth Bowes-Lyon (later the Queen and later still the Queen Mother). She resembled her so remarkably that from a few yards off and with the light behind her, you really couldn't tell them apart. It was extraordinary. Everyone said so. But she had less staying power than the Queen. She had been married to Lionel for some twenty years and knew well enough that he had an eye for the girls. But it didn't bother her. She trusted him – trusted him, that is, not to do anything *really* silly, especially now that he had a public position to uphold. She was often away in Herefordshire, near Madley, walking, riding, those sorts of things, while he was on the river in London, and so she was mercifully out of earshot of those frenzied cries, 'Leo! Leo!', coming now from her own boat, the boat that had been named after her, *Pauline*. Nor did she realise that Haselhurst, having fallen passionately in love with Yolande Holroyd, was content to leave Iseult to her own devices – those feminine devices that were spreading round and embracing her Leo.

Pauline was astonished, as well as deeply hurt, when Lionel came and asked her for a divorce. She could hardly credit that a man now entering his forties could be so bloody stupid. He was certainly no man of steel. His weakness made a mockery of their past. Once he had secretly married her for love; now in the light of publicity she was being asked to dissolve the marriage, also, allegedly, for love. What a farce! But it was also a tragedy. She would never forgive Iseult, and it astonished her that the two men, Lionel and Henry, could remain so friendly.

Of course Lionel did the gentlemanly thing, allowing Pauline to act as petitioner, and omitting Iseult from the whole sorry business. Though his family believed he spent a night with some woman hired to provide legal proof of adultery (he registered the dissolution of the marriage in *Who's Who*), the Court Service has been unable to find any record of this divorce, which seems inexplicable – it can't have been an annulment. In any event their marriage was apparently dissolved.

Haselhurst too petitioned for a divorce in the summer of 1933 so that he could be in a position to marry my Aunt Yolande. His divorce was made absolute in January 1934, and on 5 February Lionel Beaumont-Thomas gave up his political career and married Iseult Haselhurst in Kensington.

Also living in Kensington was his brother Reggie Beaumont-Thomas who, ten days later, married my grandfather's Dulcinea, Agnes May Babb.

They had a good deal in common, Henry Edward Haselhurst and Agnes May Bickerstaff. Both were born into poor, working-class families in the north of England, and left these families early on – left them as if for dead. Travelling south, they fashioned new lives for themselves with imaginary backgrounds. In one chapter of their lives, they both careered into my family before speeding on elsewhere, out of sight. If I were a fiction writer, I would arrange for them to meet, and find out how they got on. Would they be drawn from these parallel pasts into a natural intimacy, or feel awkward and be wary of each other? Perhaps they did meet: after all, one of them married a man whose brother married the other's wife. It is an oddly close, if separated, relationship. And if they did meet, would they have recognised at what point their lives had so curiously overlapped? Possibly not: which provides the fiction writer with an intriguing game to play. 'Oh, how I sometimes yearn for the easy swing of a well-oiled novel!' But I must not cheat. I must write my story without invention – or rather, I must use the characters' inventions and not my own.

Both of them appeared to be anomalies. While most people, then as now, develop an interest in their family histories, seeing in them their own places in group pictures extending over time, Henry Haselhurst and Agnes May Bickerstaff cut out their individual images from such groups and set them in different contexts and against grander backgrounds. Others might be content to find concealed layers to their identities and a new understanding of their roles within sagas of genetic patterns – continuing patterns that seemed to confer collective immortality on them. But for these two, such narrowness and repetition were not to be endured. For are we not, every one of us, the children of countless generations? And do we not therefore command almost infinite, unseen territory over which to travel – if nature is not confined by meagre parental habits?

Henry Haselhurst and Agnes May Bickerstaff denied their origins and went their ways, moving on wings of make-believe towards an unprecedented future. Neither was gifted with deep powers of imagination, talent or intelligence, but they had energy, initiative and the courage to take risks. Both were motivated by romantic and perhaps economic dreams. And both, having no children of their own, felt an urge to escape what others may have seen as their domestic destinies.

> There's a divinity that shapes our ends
> Rough-hew them as we will.

Early in the twentieth century, Frank Harris rewrote Shakespeare's lines thus:

There's a divinity rough-hews our ends
We shape it as we please.

Now, a hundred years later, the word 'divinity' might plausibly be replaced with 'biology', and the prospect of genetic engineering seen as strengthening the validity of Harris's rewritten lines. Perhaps, after all, his was a vision rather than simply a boast.

In the meantime, his biographer Philippa Pullar's life, which in no obvious way resembled the lives of her parents, may be taken as exemplifying Harris's belief in the power of the individual will and the unexpected multiplicity of choices open to us. As society in Britain, rocked by two world wars, grew more unstable, so the push of those among its poorer classes began to be more strongly felt. The adventures of Henry Haselhurst and Agnes May Bickerstaff were part of this movement, making them not so much anomalies after all, but fragments of a new social experience.

Agnes May Bickerstaff was a year younger than Haselhurst and born a hundred miles west, over the Yorkshire border in Lancashire. Both their paternal grandfathers (coincidentally given the name William) were labourers in local chemical firms. But Agnes May's mother, Robina Laurie, came from a lowlands Scottish family and her father was a 'dyker', a man who made stone dykes along the tide-swollen land above the Solway Firth. I doubt, however, if Agnes May and my grandfather ever spoke to each other of their Scottish mothers – that past was quite remote from them both during their few years together in the West End of London. In any event, Agnes May liked to believe that her Scottish ancestors were aristocrats and that she was descended from Sir Robert Laurie whose daughter, Annie Laurie, became the subject of a famous song written by her rejected suitor, William Douglas. 'And for bonnie Annie Laurie/I'll lay me down and dee.'

On 2 January 1888, Robina had married Joseph Bickerstaff, a glass-grinder, at Toxteth. She was twenty-eight, he five years younger. No member of their families came to the wedding, and Agnes May was not born for another seven and a half years. In adult life, she never mentioned these early years in the north. She appears to have been solitary. 'I thought she was an orphan,' one of her friends told me.

She lived as if she were attached to no past, but pursuing an ever-changing future. But in fact she came from a close and crowded family and was the third of four good-looking, lively sisters. The name of the eldest, Ethel Arthur Bickerstaff, suggests some gender confusion (she would later be called 'Betty'). Born in 1888, she was almost seven years older than Agnes May – and three years older than the next sister, Robina Grey (called 'Ann'). In 1900 came another extravagant name, Melville Pretoria Bickerstaff (nicknamed 'Medal'). All four sisters were born in St Helens, but each one at a different address. The Bickerstaffs moved at least five times within a dozen years, and at every house they took in lodgers – sometimes simply nephews and nieces, but increasingly apprentices at the glass company where Joseph Bickerstaff worked, as well as young men, often from the south of England (the secretary of a YMCA office in Sussex, a chap from the railways, and so on). There were always, it seems, young men, travelling men, staying at the Bickerstaffs' home while the sisters were growing up. The rent they paid enabled the family to employ a domestic servant (a big step up from the previous generation – Joseph Bickerstaff's mother could neither read nor write).

Robina Grey Bickerstaff was the first sister to marry. She suffered from a weak chest and was sent each winter to some relatives, the Baverstocks, in Thames Ditton where the climate was warmer. In October 1912, some sixteen days short of her twenty-first birthday (she made herself twenty-one on the certificate to gain legal authority), she became Mrs Arthur Edward Pennington, the wife of a twenty-seven-year-old cashier in Thames Ditton. The marriage certificate reveals that her father had by then risen to be an assistant manager at the Pilkington Glass Works in St Helens.

This marriage seems to have been a turning point in the story of the Bickerstaff family. Within a year they had all left St Helens and gathered in Southampton where Joseph, then in his forty-seventh year, started out on a new career as landlord of the Dock Hotel in Canute Road. Into this eccentric establishment they all piled: his wife Robina, their three unmarried daughters (including the eighteen-year-old Agnes May or 'Maimie' as she was called), as well as their newly married daughter, her husband and, in December 1914, a first grandson, Arthur Gordon Grey Pennington, who was born in the hotel.

The Bickerstaff story resembles the plot of an Arnold

Bennett novel: the man from the north journeying south during times of trouble and seeking to improve himself and his family in the bustling new surroundings of a modern hotel. The hotel 'is in my opinion a unique subject for a serious novel', Bennett was to write in his diary when beginning *Imperial Palace*; 'it is stuffed with human nature of extremely various kinds ... characteristic of the age ... as modern as the morning's milk'.

The Dock Hotel, though faintly oriental, was not a hotel *de luxe*. There were no thick gorgeous carpets, no temperamental barmen or chefs to unnerve you with American cocktails or French menus, no shining millionaires from the New World, no encrusted foreign royalty or, as the plot develops, no expensive and mysterious corpses. The guests do not wear faultless evening dress and never handle complicated cutlery; they are seldom oppressed by an atmosphere saturated with deference. For it is a more homely place, the Dock Hotel, made out of three houses that have been knocked together – less in line with Arnold Bennett's tremendous *Grand Babylon Hotel* than the Potwell Inn where H. G. Wells's Mr Polly ends up. It has its share, however, of 'extremely various' human nature.

Why had the Bickerstaffs made such a dramatic change? These two years leading to the war were filled with social unrest. There had been riots in the docks, a mutiny in the army, violent suffragette demonstrations, loyalist shootings in Ireland, the Marconi share scandal and strikes by miners and the transport industry that suddenly brought the country to a halt. It was worse in the north. The headlines of the *St*

Helens Reporter on 29 March 1912 biblically prophesied: 'The End in Sight'. While the Coal Mines (Minimum Wage) Bill was being debated in Parliament, the miners themselves were looting coal from the Lancashire claypits and many railway services were cut. There was fighting in the streets and one man in St Helens was killed. 'Pilkington's works close. Thousands of men thrown idle. Relief agencies at work', announced the *St Helens Reporter*. Because it relied on fuel supplies, the Pilkington Glass Works was forced to shut its gates, and Joseph Bickerstaff became one of six thousand men suddenly without a job. He hung around with his wife and three unmarried daughters hoping for re-employment, but when the King and Queen came to St Helens the following year to open the new glass works at Cowley Hill, he was not taken on. He had climbed the ladder and become an assistant manager: then the ladder had been thrown to the ground. After working at Pilkington's, man and boy, for thirty years, he was left without any chance of a job for the remainder of his life. What prospects there were lay in the south. He gathered together all his savings, sold up and took his family to Southampton.

The Dock Hotel was a public house with bedrooms. It was owned by Graves, the brewers, which appointed Joseph Bickerstaff as its landlord. This was to be a completely new career for him, but for his wife Robina, now in her early fifties, it was not so very different from managing the lodging houses in which she had lived all her married life, or even looking after other families' children in St Helens as she had done before her marriage. But Southampton itself was a very different town.

In the early Victorian days it had been a seaside resort and this southern part of the town a fashionable residential quarter. The sea came up almost to where the hotel now stood and the curve of their street traced an ancient shoreline and the arc of a once-popular bathing beach. But all this was gradually obliterated during the mid-nineteenth century with the advance of the South Western Railway (two railway lines crossed Canute Road) and the building of the Southampton docks on the mudlands. Canute Road itself was at the centre of all this development, no longer part of a residential area, but a place of active commerce. At one end of the road stood a three-storeyed Italianate block with rusticated round arches: the Terminus Station (much admired later on by John Betjeman). To the east, it ended in the sand mills at Floating Bridge Road, where a steam ferry crossed the sluggish River Itchen.

It was not a beautiful place in which to live. *Kelly's Directory of Southampton* shows Canute Road to have been simply a line of shipping agents, engineering firms, trading companies, the freight departments of Cunard and White Star, emigration offices, ice storage plants, fitters, painters, clearing houses, seamen's unions. But scattered among all these business buildings were a few taverns, cafés and small hotels.

The Bickerstaffs were to be connected with the Dock Hotel for almost twenty years. During the Second World War, it was destroyed in one of the terrible bombing raids that were to damage thousands of houses and leave Southampton a ruined place, a ghost town. Another twenty years, and the architectural historian, Nikolaus Pevsner, is walking along the 'sardonically named' Canute Road on one of his celebrated 'perambulations'. He starts off from the threadbare municipal landscape of Queen's Park with its 'grotesque monument to General Gordon'. The once busy road is now largely derelict, though many of the old buildings, sometimes unoccupied, still stand, in particular the monumental South Western Hotel, attached to the Terminus Station (later to become an 'Ocean Casino'). This had been Southampton's first great hotel, the sort of proud illuminated place, with its promise of perpetual gaiety, that warmed the heart of Arnold Bennett. 'The whole building very nearly convinces,' Nikolaus Pevsner concedes. He continues walking, past the 'poor neo-Wrenish' old Custom House, the stone-dressed Cunard office, and a few decayed relics from that era of confident expansion as far as the Canute Castle Hotel. This 'agreeable piece of whimsicality', which was there when the Bickerstaffs arrived, delights him. He is now only two hundred yards from where the Dock Hotel itself stood. He looks up, concludes from what he sees that 'there are no strong architectural reasons for proceeding further', and turns back.

I have been able to find no photographs of the Dock Hotel in the volumes on pre-war Southampton; but pictures of the docks themselves, with their handsome array of liners and steam yachts, gleaming with the promise of thrilling adventures as they lie, gently rocking on the languid waters, destined for Asia, Europe and the Americas, show why Joseph Bickerstaff was drawn from the wastes of St Helens to this prosperous region. From the Dock Hotel itself you could hear on boisterous days the flapping and jangling forest of masts from the smaller vessels and see the stir of lights and flags belonging to the great ships of the main – the China Sea, the Indian Ocean and other enticing waters leading to the uttermost ends of the earth. Agnes May, however, did not find it a glamorous place in which to live. Even as a child she had thought of herself as 'superior' to her family and was teased because of this. In her fantasies she was sometimes illegitimate, sometimes adopted, sometimes American. In any event definitely not a Bickerstaff. Travelling to the soft south of England reinforced these illusions which grew and flourished like exotic flowers in a hot house. She longed, as it were, to be transplanted, to go to London and grow into someone else. At the age of nineteen she has left Canute Road and by twenty she is married to a second lieutenant in the London Regiment, and living in Surrey. On the marriage certificate she writes that her father is dead – and indeed she never appears to have seen him or her mother again during the remaining twenty-five years of their lives. One of her nieces remembers how Agnes May's mother would increasingly search the newspapers for some mention of her. She felt sure that her missing daughter would one day dramatically hit the headlines. But, for good or bad, she was gone for ever.

For Agnes May's sisters, the Dock Hotel seems to have been rather an exciting place. In their teens and early twenties, they were a strikingly attractive group, these sisters, high-spirited, good-looking, fond of parties – especially fancy-dress parties. They loved dressing up and going out – and this was to be the tenor of their lives as they began speaking with new accents, becoming different people as they entered a middle-class life. It was perhaps hardest for the eldest sister to adapt to these new ways – she was already in her early twenties by the time the family arrived in Southampton. But the second sister (who had spent many winters in the south) adapted brilliantly, using these early fancy-dress parties as if they were rehearsals for her post-war career on the stage (where she was to perform using the name 'Ann Penn'). As for Agnes May, her future life may be seen as a fancy-dress affair, with many changes of role, many changes of cast and background.

One of the best features of the Dock Hotel, especially for the youngest sister, Medal, was the number of new faces you saw there. People were always coming and going – mostly men, of course, men with stories, men of all sorts: tinkers, tailors, soldiers, sailors . . .

Did any rich men, as well as poor, turn up there? In 1918, at the age of twenty-six, the eldest sister, Ethel Arthur Bickerstaff (now definitely called Betty), married a New Zealander, a lieutenant in the Royal Navy Volunteer Reserve named Vivian Guesdon – both of them giving the Dock Hotel as their residence. The Guesdons were to be the least well-off of all the Bickerstaff sisters. She suffered an early miscarriage, following which they had no children. After leaving the navy Vivian Guesdon worked intermittently as a marine engineer. For the last twenty years or so of his life, he seems to have been partly dependent on his wife, who managed the Anchorage Hotel, a mile or so inland from the Dock Hotel, near Southampton Cemetery. They were helped financially by her youngest sister's family. When he died in 1961, Vivian Guesdon was worth little more than a thousand pounds.

But the husband of Melville Pretoria Bickerstaff, the youngest sister Medal, was minded to be rich. True, the man she chose was a divorced gentleman, probably paying alimony, when he arrived at the Dock Hotel in the early 1920s. But Albert Rogers came from a family of quite successful shipping contractors. He owns as much on his marriage certificate, but does not admit his connections with the pork butchers at Canal Walk, Rose and Rogers, 'makers of the celebrated sausages'. He was almost twice the age of his wife, who was twenty-three when he married her in 1925. The Penningtons, the Guesdons and Bickerstaffs, all their families were at the Rogers' wedding. The only sister missing is Agnes May.

By 1925 Agnes was divorced from her first husband and had married her second husband whom she would soon be leaving to become my grandfather's mistress in the West End of London. How much of all this did her family get to hear? Almost nothing, it appears. There is only one verifiable moment of contact. In the summer of 1920, on the day of Agnes May's second marriage, her younger sister Melville Pretoria, then just turned twenty and working in London, had come to the wedding in Kensington Register Office. It must have been her steadying presence that prompted Agnes May to bring her father alive again on her marriage certificate and describe him, with only slight exaggeration, as a hotel proprietor. But after this, as Agnes May's life grows more erratic and extraordinary, all contact with her sisters and her parents ends.

She did, however, visit Southampton once. She arrived with her third husband, the small-headed, immensely tall, semi-paralysed Reggie Beaumont-Thomas in the late 1930s. They hastened on board a liner at Southampton Docks, a few hundred yards from the Dock Hotel, and sailed for the United States. It was to be a pleasure cruise, but there was little pleasure in it after Reggie fell on deck (it was claimed he slipped on a banana skin), injuring himself painfully. He was never very agile, never too steady on his feet, though he blamed the shipping company for his accident. When they got back to England, he busied himself lethargically with a legal action against the company, which eventually lapsed at the beginning of the war.

There was little chance of Agnes May visiting her sisters, the nephews and nieces she had never seen, or her mother and father when embarking at Southampton because, as she had explained to Reggie, her parents were dead and she had no family. In any event, by the late 1930s, circumstances had changed. Joseph Bickerstaff's name disappears as landlord of the Dock Hotel in 1920 and, for the next ten years his wife Robina becomes its landlady. Evidently something serious had happened. In 1925 Joseph was not with the rest of the family at his daughter Melville Pretoria's wedding. Had he left them? It seems that his health may have failed dramatically. His grandchildren did not know he was still alive while they were young, and their grandmother never spoke of him. He was admitted as a rate-aided inmate to the West End Institution which specialised in the 'observation of mental defectives' in the Dickensian-sounding district of Shamblehurst. Then, at the beginning of 1942, following a pronounced 'attack of mental illness', he was transferred to Knowle Hospital, the local 'lunatic asylum', where he was placed next to another Bickerstaff, a clergyman suffering from sexual delusions. He had heavy bruising to his chest and many cuts to his body – almost certainly the result of an air raid. After a week here, and on the very day he was to be discharged, he died, aged seventy-four, the immediate cause of his death being a heart attack.

Robina passed her retirement years with two of her daughters' families: the Guesdons at the Anchorage Hotel, and the Rogers family with their teenage son and daughter outside Southampton, at Myrtle Cottage, Brockenhurst, where she lived during her last years. She was not able to see so much of her eldest grandchild because the Penningtons had by then moved to London, and she had seen nothing of her husband Joseph. But in 1943, after her death at the age of eighty-three in St Catherine's Nursing Home at Christchurch, the family buried her next to him in Hollybrook Cemetery.*

---

*Grave number 205 in section L12. Also buried there are their daughter Ethel Arthur ('Betty') and son-in-law Vivian Guesdon.

Between her father's and mother's deaths, late in 1942, Agnes May finally parted from her husband Reggie Beaumont-Thomas. Following his fall on the boat to the United States, Reggie had been largely confined to a wheelchair. It was a horribly tedious and frustrating business for her. But she bravely refused to be imprisoned by his illness. After all, it was wartime, a time (as the newspapers often reminded their readers) to keep the spirits up. To enjoy oneself became a patriotic duty, a moral necessity. One night while she was out with an admirer, their house at Bushey was burgled, the burglars attacking Reggie, overturning his wheelchair and leaving him shocked and stranded on the floor. He seemed destined for disaster: first the rumours of infantile paralysis and 'sleepy sickness'; next the fabulous accident playing 'Rugby at Eton'; then the legendary banana skin in mid-Atlantic; and now beset by burglars in his home. When Agnes May eventually returned, he ordered her to leave. He could not stand it any longer. He would settle an allowance on her (as he had on his Parisian dancing wife); he would pay her to go away and stay away (as my grandfather had done). The pattern was by now familiar.

Where did she go? Evidently not to Southampton (I can find no entry for her in the telephone books, register of electors, or any other directory there). By the end of 1943 I have again lost her.

Around this time, the figure of Henry Haselhurst begins to slide into the mists of rumour and speculation. His last letter to my Aunt Yolande was written from the north of England in 1942 soon after he joined the Cheshire Regiment. He sends her a snapshot of himself in his uniform. Of course this is not the man she met and fell in love with ten years earlier. The photo shows a full, modestly moustached, fairly unremarkable face, with a lazy eye, almost smiling, nearly anonymous. He seems to be making the best of things whatever they are, and looks quietly confident that, somehow or other, these things will get better. And he is right. But meanwhile, despite the line of medal ribbons, the 'wings' from the Great War above them, the buttons and the regimental badges decorating his collar and hat, the picture is not quite convincing. It is the officer's hat that is at fault. It tilts towards his left eye, the good eye, and looks not so much rakish, nor even racy, as simply too large. But he will grow into it. He has been given the substantive rank of major and is stationed (though not permitted to tell my aunt this) at Caldy Manor, a not uncomfortable, red-brick, Elizabethan-style mansion, much knocked about by its recent owner, a Liverpool cotton broker.

For a good year Haselhurst and his regiment trained for combat in the pleasant woods and meadows nearby – and passed on their training to the newly formed Home Guard and Civil Defence Authorities. Their days were crammed with guard duty, drill, kit inspections and fatigues (mainly road-mending, trench-digging and potato-peeling). This routine, of which he sometimes complained to women and children, had a rhythm that was strangely comforting. To prepare themselves for war the men handed in their rifles. They were then given sten guns and mortars which needed months of nervous tactical handling in the fields. They moved from draughty huts into draughty tents, and then back again into draughty huts. It was an invigorating programme. Their main enemy over all this time, this marking of time, was not the Germans but their own boredom. They longed to meet a German, even an Italian would do.

Finally, they were judged to be ready for active service. On 9 September 1943, now a temporary lieutenant-colonel and as officer in charge of the Thirtieth Battalion of the Cheshire Regiment, Haselhurst embarked with his men on the *Athlone Castle.* They were being sent to North Africa which had recently fallen to the Allies. Much that they did over the next eighteen months was then, of course, pretty well top secret. Now it can be told. From Algiers they struggled into a transit camp on the windswept plain of Blida from where, being overwhelmed by several unprecedented floods, they quickly moved up to Sousse where their soldierly work could begin in earnest. From hidden parts of their heavy baggage, deeply concealed, the Battalion Dance Band unwrapped its armoury of musical instruments (chiefly a piano and some drums) and struck up a wonderful din around a huge camp fire that Haselhurst had ordered to be prepared. During the next three weeks their morale was continually sustained by these open-air concerts and dances under the stars, also by drinks parties and race meetings which, with a little light shooting in defence of their rations, 'taught the men to be alert and self-reliant'. In short, to keep on their toes. Altogether it was capital fun, as was a hard-fought football match against the Irish Guards at Bizerte (though they lost 0–2).

Excitement soared even higher when, in mid-December, battling against the weather, under darkness and in heavy rain, they joined a convoy sailing up the Mediterranean to Taranto. Next morning they pushed on by slow train to Salerno where, three months earlier, the Eighth Army had begun its invasion of Italy. They started their duties here immediately by opening a soup kitchen which Haselhurst himself, as it were, superintended (you need to read this sentence aloud for the full flavour). There were other employments too for the Cheshires (such as keeping a weather eye on the docks and a sharp look out for air raids). But the single most dangerous hostility (it covered their uniforms and instruments with an awful grey ash) was to be the eruption of Vesuvius that March.

Eight days after the Fifth Army entered Rome, Haselhurst led his band of Cheshires into the city. They had 'received the compliment', the regimental history reveals, of doing garrison duty there, parading outside Allied headquarters ('vital installations') to general applause (one general went so far as to call them 'a bloody fine crowd'). But their time was not without hazards. For example, Mussolini's ornate building in which they were billeted proved 'highly dangerous', having no handrail on the stairs. Their other duties were 'heavy' but 'miscellaneous'. They raised pigs and fowls on a farm outside Rome, and helped the farmer grow his grapes, melons and tomatoes. Haselhurst's 'constructive ideas' were singled out as being of special help to the Pioneer Section which equipped one of the theatres in Rome for additional dancing. 'Constant vigilance was needed' over finding schemes to equip the men for the threat of civilian life to come. To this end they took lessons in elementary bricklaying, carpentry and motor mechanics. Everyone had to keep mentally fit too, which is why they held plenty of sports meetings. Rome, so people said, was a beautiful city, but it was also a damn warm spot, as the Cheshires discovered, in which to play cricket. Yet 'nothing pleased him [Haselhurst] more than to be present and take part in these many functions', the *Oaktree Journal* records.

The *Cheshire Regimental History of the Second World War* contains a photograph of Haselhurst sporting his Royal Flying Corps 'wings' from the First World War (their outline repeated in the smiling curve of his mouth and razor-thin moustache above a monocle suspended from his neck, like an exclamation mark dramatically cancelled by the diagonal slash of his Sam Browne). These travels with the Cheshires since leaving Blighty might not have held the escapist rapture and high romance of his air adventures, but the nail-biting football matches and tense race meetings, the continual swimming and dancing were rather terrific. He seemed to feel most at home when travelling abroad like this and treated the men of the Cheshires as if they were his own family.

He was also absorbed into an Italian family with whom he had been billeted, and this became part of his own preparation for civilian life. He had got to know the nineteen-year-old, dark-haired Palmina Abbagnano, and her younger sister Mariolina, through their aunt, who was

English. The two sisters, daughters of an Italian philosopher, were greatly taken with him, especially when he came to dinner one evening with General Alexander (the Cheshires were acting as his 'flagship guards' in Rome). Haselhurst was now in his fifty-second year – almost three times Palmina's age and five years older than her mother. But he didn't look it, and they didn't know it. So where was the harm? It seemed as if the years had rolled back and those pale, indecisive episodes with Cicely, Iseult and Yolande were all cancelled. On 5 April 1945, a month before VE Day, at the military station of the Central Mediterranean Forces in Rome, he married Palmina and began a new life.

It began well. Six weeks later he was sailing back to England and then travelling up to Cheshire with his regiment and glamorous young wife. On 1 October, having exceeded the age limit for the reserves, he finally left the army. Altogether he had passed over half his adult life as a soldier and airman – almost twenty years, and they had been happy years. Military life lent him an objective and the very uniforms he wore, with their decorations and insignia, appeared to clothe him with a convincing identity. He was granted the honorary rank of lieutenant-colonel and for the rest of his life was known simply as 'the Colonel' (as he had been 'the Captain' following the First World War). He collected more medals and on his retirement was made an Officer of the British Empire (OBE). 'We have lost not only a grand commanding officer,' recorded the *Cheshire Regimental History*, 'but also a good friend.'

Fortunately the Colonel already had some good friends in Cheshire, in particular the Blond family whom he had met there in the early days of the war. Neville Blond was a wealthy textile manufacturer (a specialist in rubber clothing) who had developed an interest in the arts (he became chairman of the English Stage Company) and who was shortly to be appointed UK trade adviser to the United States. He was happy pursuing his successful career; but he was far from happy at home. His wife Eileen had married him in 1927 on the rebound from an intense love affair, and by the time Haselhurst turned up at their large house in Cheshire, Neville had gone south to live with a girl he was to marry in 1944. There were two sons living in Cheshire with their mother, one of whom, to my surprise, I realised that I knew.

Anthony Blond was a celebrated, rather risqué London publisher at the time I began writing books in the 1960s. His authors ranged from Harold Robbins and Simon Raven to Gillian Freeman and Jean Genet. When I located Anthony, now living in France, he gave me an introduction to his brother Peter (who works at Sotheby's) and together they helped me to understand something of Haselhurst's post-war life.

The Blond brothers' memories of Haselhurst are very similar to those of the Dracopoli boys, Iseult's children, in the 1920s. He is their hero too: a tremendously exciting, funny, adventurous man who made their days vivid with possibilities. It seemed to them as if Biggles, the ace flier and 'air detective' created by W. E. Johns, whose gripping yarns they read each month in *Modern Boy*, had come to life and entered their world. When they were out with him, listening to his exploits as they all whizzed around the country on their bicycles, they felt as if they too were caught up in strange adventures and had become Biggles's daredevil pals, Algy or Bertie or, best of all, his tough, loyal commando-companion Ginger. This was the best of war.

These had been exhilarating days for the boys. So when Haselhurst came back from Italy and, with his wife Palmina, rented an apartment in their mother's huge and rather empty house in Cheshire, they were overjoyed. He was such a wonderful mentor, gentle, firm, informative, encouraging: a father figure. They infinitely preferred him to their remote, real father Neville Blond whom, to their delight, Haselhurst nicknamed 'the Bullfrog'.

Hasel did everything the boys expected of him. He got a fast car, an Allard, and he fitted up and restored one of his pre-war boats for more adventuring at sea. It was not the motor yacht *Llanthony* which he shared with Lionel Beaumont-Thomas in the 1930s (on to which he had invited my Aunt Yolande and even my father for weekends). *Llanthony* had been acquired by the government in 1939 and became one of the famous fleet of 'little ships' – mud-hoppers, sailing yachts and pleasure steamers – that ferried their way under heavy German bombardment back and forth between the English coast and Dunkirk, rescuing British soldiers from the beach (*Llanthony* took back 280 soldiers). Then, after the war she was given back to Lionel's widow, Iseult Beaumont-Thomas, who sold her to Lord Astor of Hever, raising images of her future use by his most enticing and notorious guest, Christine Keeler.*

Such images, even if false, would not have amused Colonel Haselhurst. For all his free and easy ways, he was something of a puritan. Though he had never mentioned her in his letters to my aunt, he had become rather specially fond of Eileen, Neville Blond's divorced wife. She was an Italian, like his wife, which was convenient. But he couldn't hide his disapproval of her love affairs – nor of her remarriage after the war – indeed he was inclined to blame Eileen for her bad influence on Palmina.

Llanthony was commandeered during the Dunkirk evacuation by Rear-Admiral Robert Timbrell of the Royal Canadian Navy. He had been surprised to find that she was a gentleman's yacht, ill-equipped for naval duty, her only weapon the 1914 Colt on Timbrell's leather belt. With a crew of two civilian diesel engineers from London Transport and six lumberjacks from Newfoundland, she set course for Dunkirk with orders to anchor off the beach and take on as many troops as possible. 'It was a very shallow beach,' Admiral Timbrell remembered, 'and at low tide, the water went out a long way. We were being shelled by the Germans [and] the town was in flames . . . We could take about 120 on each trip and our instructions were to return as soon as we were loaded. We did that for a couple of trips. Then, on the third or fourth trip, we got bombed . . . We were hit on the fo'c'sle. I lost about five of our crew and both my anchors snapped . . . the fuel pipes were severed so that both engines died. We drifted on to the beach. It was a sunny afternoon and there were shells falling all the way down the beach with thousands of soldiers asking to be taken back to England. It was day four of the evacuation and a stream of ships were going in and out. We drove some trucks into the water to form a small jetty. Then, at high tide, we could go alongside the trucks and men could walk on top of them and jump aboard . . .

As they grew up, the Blond brothers, Anthony and Peter, began looking at Hasel in a new way. Although he remained a generous friend to them during their adolescence (taking them both to France on his yacht and letting them 'bugger up the boat' without too much fuss), he did not seem to have any close and lasting friends among the adults. He was gregarious, but also somewhat solitary. Sometimes he gave the impression of being proud, even cold or at least distant, and beneath his cheerful demeanour, they noticed, lay a film of bitterness and resentment. This usually came to the surface

---

'[A sergeant] asked if he could help and I told him to get a Bren-gun carrier and drive it out as far as he could in the water until the engine stopped so that I could use it to anchor by. That is what he did and my two civilian diesel engineers repaired the fuel pipes, got the capstan going and winched us off. They put a plate over my bombed fo'c'sle and we sailed back to England . . .

'Our last trip was the tightest. The Germans had started to enter the town and to close a ring round Dunkirk. There was no way we could return any more. Back in Portsmouth I had a job to find anyone who would take over *Llanthony* from me. She was beaten up with bullet holes in her funnels.'

In 1952 she was bought from Lord Astor by Baron Kronacher's Société pour l'Exportation du Sucre, registered in Antwerp, and eighteen years later passed on to the Yvomarcos Shipping Company. From 1985 to 1993, renamed the *Golden Era*, she cruised between Greece and Turkey as a charter yacht. In 1995 she was discovered lying in Rhodes Harbour in a dilapidated state, and put to sail on one engine by Ms Nicola McGrail who took her to the Netsel Marina at Marmaris in Turkey where, after extensive renovation, she became a showpiece. She returned to British waters, with all her original fittings, for the Diamond Anniversary of Dunkirk Little Ships in June 2000.

when he spoke about women. He was curiously censorious, even rude, about his wife when speaking to the boys. He had married Palmina, he told them, in order 'to have a fuck'; and she had married him, he added, as a way of getting to England.

In 1948, after three years of marriage, he began divorce proceedings against Palmina on the grounds of her adultery. It was difficult sometimes to understand his attitude. Often he appeared to be the complaisant husband, but then would suddenly come out with bursts of hostility. Indeed he had little good to say about any of his wives. Yolande he never mentioned. She was one of his secrets, like his parents and the first sixteen years of his life which he still embroidered with grand fantasies. Once, coming nearer to the truth perhaps, he remarked that, having successfully escaped the 'love' of his elderly mother, he had no wish to be 'possessed' by any woman. So, in a sense, his divorce from Palmina, which was made absolute at the beginning of 1949, was a relief. He resumed friendly relations with her family and was best man at her sister's wedding. Palmina herself went on to marry an estate agent and have two sons whom she named Peter and Anthony, after the Blond brothers. She was, in her own right, a rich woman, and perhaps this was the source of Haselhurst's resentment. He was no longer a gentleman 'of independent means' as he claimed his father had been, as he wished his father had been.

He returned to London and moved into Dolphin Square, a ten-storeyed, red-brick apartment block in Pimlico that features in the novels of C. P. Snow. Also moving in at the same time was the novelist Angus Wilson. His biographer describes Dolphin Square as being 'the height of chic'.

> It occupied over seven acres, had its own private gardens and some fine river views. The furnishings were Art Deco, there was a restaurant with an orchestra and a view of the swimming pool, and each room had a radio with a Bakelite control which could be switched to the Home, Light or Third Programme. The décor reminded Angus pleasantly of his sea-voyage to South Africa, and the nautical theme was echoed in the names of the houses: Grenville, Beatty, Howard, Hood . . .
>
> It was and is inhabited by a wide range of characters – diplomats, politicians, con men, artists, spies, call girls, minor royals and many others with good reason to wish for trouble-free, well-run anonymity.

Angus Wilson and Henry Haselhurst both courted anonymity, its peace and independence, having cut free from their families and being known now by surnames that differed from those of their parents. But, within the same building, they occupied very different worlds. Angus Wilson's flat looked inwards on to the private gardens where he sat creating extravagant, macabre scenes. Haselhurst's flats, first in Drake House then in Nelson House, both looked out along the river where his auxiliary schooner, *Black Pearl*, lying at anchor nearby, could carry him away, anytime, anywhere, like one of the characters, Swallow or Amazon, in Arthur Ransome's adventures.

He used Dolphin House as an office as well as his home and employed a widow, the devoted Mary Gardner, who was twenty-one years younger than himself, as his secretary. After bumping into him in the street one day his ex-stepson Jack Dracopoli, recently demobbed from the RAF, went to work for Haselhurst and noticed what a clever engineer he was. During the long fuel crisis after the war, he introduced himself to several laundries, rearranging their systems of burners so that they operated more efficiently – he was paid a percentage of what they saved in fuel costs. Later he designed the drums for the 'four-hour cleaner' which was popular with housewives during the 1950s. But he took little pride in his engineering ingenuity. Listed as 'Colonel Hazlehurst OBE', he was now a member of the Royal Thames Yacht Club in Knightsbridge, the Royal Solent Yacht Club on the Isle of Wight, the Royal Motor Yacht Club at Poole in Dorset and the Royal Air Force Yacht Club. He enjoyed passing his time with these boat people, ex-officers, 'company directors' – high fliers who had no need to be tethered to land jobs.

Women still found him attractive. Even in his sixties there was still a boyish charm to his enthusiasms. He would regularly take women out to theatres and restaurants in London, and for cruises along the river and round the coast, but these relationships were flirtatious rather than sexual. He once confessed to one of the Blond boys that despite his three wives and innumerable girlfriends, he had had comparatively little sexual experience – very little in the context of 1960s mores.

On 12 March 1974 Haselhurst turned seventy. He would spend more of his time indoors during his seventies. A friend had given him a red setter called Gary with whom he played extravagant games of hide and seek in the apartment – the sort of games that he and I have been playing. When Gary died, he was given another dog, a chocolate-coloured poodle, Piper. It seems an unlikely breed of dog for the Colonel, but like my Aunt Yolande he appears to have been fond of all dogs. Putting his black patch over one eye, he would increasingly sit in the window of his apartment during the evenings watching the boats, criticising their manoeuvres and, like Dylan Thomas's Captain Cat, recall many glorious fictional episodes from past days. 'I can find no evidence that he was involved in yacht racing,' writes the archivist of the Royal Thames Yacht Club. Yet his mantelpiece and tables glittered with silver cups and medals which were continually polished up by his stories. His secretary Mary Gardner's young niece, Sally, loved being taken to Dolphin Square and listening to these stories. Once upon a time, she thought, he must have been like Little Lord Fauntleroy. He was so quick-witted, such fun; no wonder that, with his strange eccentricities (he cleaned his teeth with a pair of tweezers) he seemed like an aristocrat in an old adventure book, a far-off romance. Once he took Sally and her aunt across the Channel all the way to France. They could have got off, gone anywhere, started a new life. It was an oddly exciting game – and in some sense (though she did not know this) it was what he had done with his own life.

When I spoke to Sally Harris and outlined some of Haselhurst's background, I could hear that she found what I told her difficult to believe. She did not want to disengage herself from the spell of his long-remembered tales. He was so wonderfully convincing and made the world a more interesting place.

What made him all the more exciting was the hidden part of his life. There was something mysterious about him. He didn't like being photographed or asked direct questions by children about his own childhood. But he gave them clues sometimes. When, very occasionally, he referred to his mother, he called her 'Mama' which was obviously very upper-class. Perhaps he was illegitimate – the son of an Irish aristocrat. He had let fall one or two hints in that direction. He had, too, a gold ring with a strange Celtic seal which he never denied was his family crest. Each month, too, he received through the post a cheque from an unknown source. 'They pay him to keep away,' his secretary Mary Gardner remarked to her niece. But who did and why? He was often abroad on his boat and several times made mysterious journeys to Guernsey, visiting someone there and coming back grave-faced. Could it be that his real father lived in exile there? Or was he being sent to Guernsey on secret missions? Then there were the telephone calls, a good number of which, he acknowledged, came from his friend Field Marshal Lord Montgomery. Sally Harris and her young cousins eventually decided that he was almost certainly a spy. Such speculations created a luminous atmosphere around him. And they gained thrilling credibility when, in the 1960s, William Vassall was jailed for spying after secret documents and a miniature camera were discovered in a concealed compartment of his flat in Dolphin Square. What a nest the place was!

It transported him, too, from all those meagre connections with the Haselhursts of Beverley – until, that is, falling seriously ill in the mid-1970s, a genetic connection pulled him back to them. He discovered that he was suffering from prostate cancer, which had killed his father and, recently, his brother Roland. In the summer of 1975 he was operated on at St Philip's Hospital in Sheffield Street, near the Royal College of Surgeons. Peter Blond went to see him there. There was something special he wished to say. Mary Gardner, Haselhurst's secretary, had been with him for some thirty years, always looking after his business, sometimes looking after him. She had come to work for him in her early thirties and was now in her early sixties. Peter knew how devoted she had been to him. If Haselhurst died, she would be left without an income and without status. He must not let this happen. He must marry her as soon as possible. There had been some talk of their marriage; now there must be some action. This was what Peter Blond told him.

Lying in his bed, very weak after his operation, Haselhurst listened to this suggestion agreeably enough. 'I'll do it some time,' he promised. But it was obvious that he would do nothing – he was not well enough and also perhaps not keen enough. He had not troubled to make a will, to consider what would happen to Mary, or really anything else, after he died and the game was over. It was not quite his style. Mary herself must have realised this and in self-defence had begun saying, half as a joke, that she would never marry someone who had already been 'used' by so many women. It became clear to Peter Blond that, to do what was right, he must organise it all himself.

247

The marriage ceremony took place beside Haselhurst's bed in the hospital ward, with the surgeon, some nurses, and the driver of a car Peter Blond had hired to bring along the Registrar. Peter himself brought champagne for everyone, and one of the nurses lent Mary her ring. It was an oddly moving ceremony. When it came to filling in the marriage certificate, Mary gave Nelson House now as her address and revealed that her father had been a 'dining car conductor' on the trains. Haselhurst said his residence these days was St Philip's Hospital and asked the Registrar to put 'Independent Means' against his father's profession. Then it came to the signing of the certificate. They propped him up against the pillows, they put a pen in his hand, they held the certificate against a hard board for him; and he began to write his name. But he could not do it. There was what might possibly be an 'H' and then perhaps an 'a'. But after that, where the spelling of his assumed name and his family name part, his handwriting gives out. There is a faint squiggle, then it stops.

The Registrar had not been very willing to conduct this unusual ceremony. Puffed up in his brief authority, he had put all manner of bureaucratic difficulties in the way – and now he had an early train to catch. He examined his watch; he examined Haselhurst's signature; and he decided it would not do. It was inadequate. He therefore refused to pronounce them man and wife – and said he must leave with the wedding unaccomplished. He had warned them all this was highly irregular, and now concluded that it was officially impossible. Again Haselhurst tried to write – but was he really trying? Peter Blond believed he was, and told the

Registrar that he would make an official complaint if he left the proceedings incomplete – indeed he would not allow the driver to take him to the railway station. He would miss his train. So the Registrar gave in, annotated the certificate twice in the margin – and everyone drank champagne.

The surgeon had already informed Mary Haselhurst that there was no possibility of her husband recovering and so, towards the end of August, she removed him from the hospital and took him to the 'Hostel of God' on the north side of Clapham Common. This was the forerunner of the hospice movement in Britain, founded by the Sisters of the Poor in the late nineteenth century and named after the Hotel Dieu in Paris. By the 1970s, it occupied four substantial eighteenth-century houses looking down on London and the Thames. It was run by the formidably autocratic, eighty-year-old Sister Magdalene and her company of nuns of the Order of St Margaret who specialised in caring for those who were dying of cancer.

In many ways this was a fitting place for Haselhurst to end his days. These houses, with their spacious gardens and conservatories, had once belonged to wealthy gentlemen and been visited by Pepys and Evelyn, Tennyson and Browning. They still retained the atmosphere of private residences. The hostel had royal patrons, too, who would sometimes pay visits when they were in the neighbourhood.

The Hostel of God had a second name: the National Free Home for the Dying.* It existed outside the National Health

---

*It is now called Trinity Hospice.

Service and was dependent on private donations for its free care. But the mid-1970s was not a favourable period in its history. Though the nuns were practised at alleviating the anguish of dying and at changing a patient's attitude to death, they were falling behind the times in medical treatment. 'We have done our best,' said Sister Magdalene. 'We must not cling to the past.' But it was not until 1977 that they were able to leave, and the hospice went on to benefit from developments in palliative care. When Haselhurst was there, the official history records, there was not enough money to buy new equipment 'and visitors were sometimes shocked by its absence'.

Haselhurst died at the Hostel of God on 12 September 1975. He was aged eighty-one. Because he had made no will and the circumstances of his marriage were so peculiar, probate took over six months to prove. But his wife, who had looked after his business for so long, managed everything very competently, and the final value of his estate at a little below £35,000 was surprisingly modest – she was herself to leave four times this amount when she died some years later.

Haselhurst was cremated later that month and his ashes scattered at sea where they could move with the tides upon the living waters, with the weather and the winds, all over the world, free from the imprisoning ground of fact.

Almost the last library that invited me to speak on autobiography and family memoirs was the one my aunt and father used in Surrey. I drove down in the late afternoon, remembering the journey I had made so soon after my aunt's death, and stopped at the cemetery to look at her gravestone. It was surrounded now by other gravestones – a village of the dead – but looked good, I thought, with the evening sun lighting up its Shakespearean words of farewell. As I walked back along the green pathway towards St Mary's Church, I wondered what she would have thought of my search for Haselhurst and the discoveries I had made about this man she loved and, for so long, hoped to marry. It was impossible to know.

That evening in the library I spoke a little about my aunt and also my father. A few people in the audience had known them by sight or by eccentric reputation – even my father's dog came in for some generous criticism. Towards the end of the discussion I asked, as I had so many times elsewhere, if anyone knew anything about Agnes May Beaumont-Thomas: and suddenly a woman at the back of the room stood up and said yes, she did know of her. I felt a frisson of excitement as I made plans to see her later at her home.

Sarah Constantine had married into the family of the one original Beaumont-Thomas who had fallen off my list – Lionel and Reggie's manly, almost equine sister Irene. She lived only a mile from where my aunt and father lived. And she knew Agnes May by reputation – Reggie she used to see at Brighton after they had separated. She liked him. He was a kindly uncle. But he had, she noticed, a very short attention span and would grow quickly irritable if people made demands on him. He was lazy and rather immature: his women and cars were like toys – dolls and Dinkies. He wanted an easy life and, though still well off, was becoming concerned about money (he didn't like people using his telephone). The trouble with the Beaumont-Thomases, she indicated, was the very opposite of that in my own family: they simply had too much money, many of them. She leafed through some family albums. The pictures were often filled by a curious obstruction, the people being pushed to one side by vast cars – in much the same manner as my own family albums were dominated by huge dogs. Sometimes there were no human beings to be seen at all in these Beaumont-Thomas records – just an elbow or an ankle in the margins. In other photographs they cowered inside or lurked behind these monstrous cars which were Reggie's passion.

Sarah Constantine was sure that Agnes May returned to London after leaving Reggie. So I recommenced my search by looking through London telephone directories from the early 1940s. It seemed a somewhat random trawl, inspecting these ranks of subscribers, but quite soon I caught sight of her. By 1944 she was back in the West End and living at 58 Buckingham Palace Road, an apartment block not far from Victoria Station. The building no longer exists, but this was patently an address of high respectability. There were ladies' hairdressers, French cleaners, antique shops, confectioners and restaurants nearby – and then, perhaps more dubiously, the Central Association for Mental Welfare and the rather drastically named World Prohibition Federation. The building itself contained almost fifty flats (Agnes May lived in number 43) and they were mostly occupied by retired clergymen, high-ranking officers and foreign diplomats, with a sprinkling of well-connected widows (Mrs Bingham-Bird, the Hon. Mrs Eveleigh-de-Moleyns) and a few late-flowering debutantes from the country. In short, it was an irreproachable place.

But Agnes May does not stay there long. Before the end of the 1940s she leaves these bishops and brigadiers, these admirals and ambassadors of Buckingham Palace Road, and reappears at 37 Ennismore Gardens, in Knightsbridge – the very address at which my stepfather Edy Fainstain was meeting his mistress, Mrs Hanbury. Perhaps this odd coincidence gives a clue to Agnes May's status there. But again, she does not stay long – just a couple of years. Then she is off and I lose her once more. I cannot tell where she is heading because I do not know in what year she died and have been unable to find her will. Did she, like Haselhurst, omit to make a will or have I simply been unable to locate it? I have ploughed laboriously through twenty-five years following her separation from Reggie to see if she remarried, and checked if there is a Beaumont-Thomas in the lists of wills over this period. I abandoned my search at the time she would have reached her mid-seventies, having found nothing. But there is one person I know who might be able to turn up something.

David Sutton is a carefully bearded, eternally youthful, radically minded, softly-spoken-yet-eloquent socialist gentleman, a football and manuscripts scholar, well known in Reading (where he is chairman of the Labour Council) and in Texas. By training he is a librarian and works as director of research projects at the University of Reading Library. Two of these research projects have been sponsored by the Strachey Trust, a charity created in the early 1970s by Lytton Strachey's sister-in-law, Alix Strachey. I am one of its founder-trustees and for twenty years have watched David Sutton steer these difficult projects to success. One of them is a Location Register of English Literary Manuscripts and Letters covering the eighteenth to the twentieth century. The other is even more forbidding: an information database of copyright holders (compiled jointly with the University of Texas). Copyright in published writings persists for seventy years after the author's death and, since there is no legal requirement to register it, the identities of the living owners is all too often lost. The only sure way of tracing a copyright owner is to follow the trail through a series of wills made over these seventy posthumous years. So David Sutton and his team are often at First Avenue House in Chancery Lane where the Court Service now keeps wills, and they have become expert at digging them out of the obscure past.

I had few qualms about misusing David Sutton's time. He likes a challenge and has a good-natured passion for solving other people's problems – and he solved mine. One day he telephoned to say that he thought he had found her, under the name Agnes Thomas. Next day I went back to First Avenue House and checked the entry. She had the right initials and was the right age. It had to be her. I ordered a copy of the will.

Agnes May died in Worthing at the end of 1974. She was in her eightieth year. Her will is an unusually detailed

document, an inventory of objects carefully marked out for
their new owners: a candlestick for one; some carpet runners
for another; a wastepaper basket for a third. There are
precise sums of money, ranging from twenty-five pounds to
two hundred pounds, reserved for her doctor, the porter at
the apartment block where she had been living, a secretary in
her solicitors' office and people she knew in the old racy days
at Bushey and in London. And she makes amendments to
these amounts in codicils. She, who has been a go-getter all
her life and never had a job, has prepared for herself another
role in death: that of the patron and benefactor. Her pages
are covered with donations to charities: to an old people's
home, to the Fire Service Benevolent Fund, to the Sussex
Constabulary (Charitable) Fund, to the Royal Society for the
Prevention of Cruelty to Animals, to the Royal National
Institution for the Preservation of Life from Shipwreck, and
others, several others. Her charitable gestures are flung wide.
But 'I have made no provision in this my will,' she writes, 'for
my Husband who is a man of Independent means and
deserted me in 1942.'

In her sisters' wills there are gifts to one another and to
their nephews and nieces.* But, though Worthing is only fifty
miles from Southampton (and a mere ten miles from Hove
where her sister 'Ann Penn' died in 1970), Agnes May has

---

*From these documents I was able to make the Bickerstaff family tree at
the end of this book, and to locate one of Agnes May's nieces who lent me
the photograph of her mother 'Medal' with 'Maimie' which appears among
the illustrations.

still never met these children, probably does not know their names, and makes instead a donation to the National Society for the Prevention of Cruelty to Children. Unlike her three sisters, who have worked steadily all their lives, she has taken risks, gone from one man to another, spent their money, cut her losses, gambled and lived as if there were no tomorrow. But when tomorrow came and the men left, she has found it difficult to keep up her standard of living which must have been why she moved from London. At her death her estate is valued at £14,000 – on the whole less than that of her sisters' families. But all of them, and their families, have risen above their parents' generation and are estate agents, company directors, colonels' ladies – or they have gone to the United States and made history there. They are no longer recognisable as 'working class'.*

Many people feel a reluctance to make wills – a reluctance

---

*Agnes May's great-niece, Penelope Margaret Ann Pennington (born 1938), however, appears to have had a more adventurous life. At Corfe Castle, in 1956, embroidering her surname to Grey-Pennington and declaring herself to be an actress, she married John Alexander Cumnock Forbes-Sempill – and almost landed in the ranks of the aristocracy. Had she remained married, she would have found herself styled as Lady Forbes of Craigievar, wife to the twelfth baronet, with a family motto ('Watch'!), a coat of arms involving muzzled gules, a crest displaying 'a cock proper', and supporters that featured a bear and a lion rampant. She would also have settled with these distinctions to live in Kirkcudbrightshire, where her great-great-grandfather, Thomas Laurie, had worked as a dyker. Unfortunately, after a protracted divorce that eventually omitted co-respondents, the marriage was dissolved in 1964 and, under one name and another, she was free to pursue further adventures.

to which Haselhurst succumbed. But Agnes May apparently enjoyed making an inventory of her acquisitions (they are like his silver cups and medals). There are over seventy items and they tell the story of her life, only part of which I can decipher. Among her mirrors and lights, the cocktail cabinet and tallboy, are those Lalique glass decorations which my grandfather gave her in the late 1920s: the vases, lamps and bowls, the ashtray with surrounding birds and 'smoke-coloured' scent bottle with apple-blossom stopper which have survived almost fifty years. But, so far as I can see, there are no family albums and nothing from her very early years – the years that she has denied. Two other items catch my attention: 'My Oil painting half length Portrait of a Lady in blue dress by Rolin [sic] Goodwin' and 'The water colour Portrait in silver frame in my lounge'. If I can find one of these portraits I will at last see what she looked like.

There are three chief executors of her will: Mrs Vera Wall, who lived near her in Worthing; Mrs Patricia Ellegard who came from London; and Agnes May's solicitor. Each of them receives £2,000 (equivalent to ten thousand pounds at the end of the century) in addition to an assembly of gifts. I decided that I would try to find the solicitor first, hoping that his firm may have kept some files of Agnes May's papers.

It is extremely unusual for a solicitor who is appointed executor of a will and whose company charges fees for the administration of that will to receive money and gifts – indeed it would not be permitted today. The practice has changed its name and its address since Agnes May's death, but I was able to track it down. Agnes May's solicitor, though long retired, was still alive, they told me, but he lived in a nursing home now and would probably be unable to help. While one of the clerks looked in the storeroom for any lingering Agnes May files (none would be found) I wrote a letter to the solicitor's wife.

She is rather intrigued and then perhaps a little perplexed by what I tell her. I explain in my letter that Agnes May, being extremely grateful for the legal work her husband did for her in the last difficult years of her life, had left him several presents (actually six champagne glasses and fifteen red Venetian wine glasses, a Queen Anne table, a Lalique vase with thorns, a hippopotamus ashtray and so on – but I do not specify these items, suddenly aware that they might resemble a list of indictments). When we speak to each other on the telephone, she grows curious – and then somewhat incredulous. What exactly had this woman left her husband? I begin to chronicle the gifts. But she knows of no champagne glasses – has never seen them. Surely I must be mistaken. I change direction and ask whether she ever met Mrs Beaumont-Thomas herself, but she has no memory of her ('he never discussed his clients with me'), and nor, she adds, has her husband any memories – she has read him my letter. When I ask her whether, nevertheless, he might possibly remember her oil portrait in a blue dress, she answers for him, her voice rising slightly, saying that, since he never visited her apartment, he could not have seen it. I do not press her further. It is a long time ago – over a quarter of a century. So we end our conversation cheerfully enough.

To find out something of the next executor, Mrs Vera Wall, I decided to go down to Worthing. Maggie and I were spending a weekend nearby, so we started early and, a finger on the police street map which the West Sussex County Librarian had sent us, negotiated our way through roundabouts and along one-way systems to the eleventh floor of a car-park tower – then raced through cascading rain to the Worthing Reference Library. Here we took shelter and stationed ourselves for the day's work.

I am not a fluent worker. The researcher and the writer are never the same person. Their temperaments and motives are different – the writer seldom seems to know what he wants and cannot give clear instructions to the researcher. It is not an easy partnership: it is a dance in the dark. While I am tunnelling deep in my research, I dream of the writing to come as if it were an ascent into sunlight. I long to be arranging the facts I have found into coherent and imaginative patterns, telling stories, recreating worlds. But then, when I actually come to the writing, and am a stationary figure at a desk, in a bed; when those empty pages, these empty pages, confront me, I feel restless and impatient. Am I not getting slower? Is there not less time? I must get a move on. I look back nostalgically at those exciting detective days when I was on the road, in the air, off to all sorts of places, roaming the country, picking up clues and signs, making some of the discoveries I need to recreate these lost lives (and recreating, perhaps, my own life too). Why did I not relish the pursuit more at the time? Partly, I think, because these bits and pieces I call my discoveries, when I actually dig them up, present themselves as problems I may never solve. A pile of odds and ends – how can I connect them all? The connections are made in the writing, and what is unknown, even unknowable, may be, as the biographer Hilary Spurling has suggested, key elements in a biographical design, like the empty areas in lace which are part of a pattern, or like those dark holes in space which hold secrets to what one can see. Until I can find a design that makes sense of everything, including what is not found, my discoveries are no more than moments of light which briefly illuminate the outlines of dark shadows. Initially I can detect nothing more than a worrying jumble of shapes. So I am an anxious worker: anxious over research, anxious within my writing – with spasms of unexpected happiness when I seem to make connections and the partnership works.

Also I am not methodical. I work by instinct. Certainly I have ends in view. But I do not know how to reach them. My plan at Worthing Reference Library was to discover when Agnes May arrived in the town, locate her addresses and go to look at them, and also find anyone who knew her, in particular Mrs Vera Wall to whom she left that half-length 'Portrait of a Lady in blue dress'.

The Worthing Reference Library has electoral registers, street directories up to 1975 (when Kelly's went bankrupt), intermittent old telephone books, microfilm copies of local newspapers – all of which may be useful. It is a well-ordered library, but all reference libraries arrange their material rather differently and as I entered and glanced round, I had the sensation of being a traveller without a compass. Maggie asked where she should go now, what I would like her to do, and I gestured vaguely towards the shelves while ordering some old telephone books from the basement. After a badly choreographed hour, we had not progressed very far. There is no notice of Agnes May's death in the *Herald* or *Gazette*, and no attention is paid to her charitable gifts, though these newspapers enjoy chastening their readers with luxurious descriptions of other people's generosity. As for Mrs Vera Wall (who lives with her son or husband Stephen Wall), she left Worthing a couple of years after Agnes May died. I already knew Agnes May's last address from her will and could see from the map that it was not far from the library. The sun was now shining and Maggie, anxious to escape from such haphazard and lacklustre work, volunteered to go in search of it and also visit the art gallery to see if Robin Goodwin's *Portrait of a Lady in a Blue Dress* was hanging on the wall.

I bent over the street directories and electoral registers plotting Agnes May's movements and did not notice the vast storm tumbling around outside – until, two hours later, a drenched, dismal and dripping figure came to a halt next to me. It was Maggie, back from her 'field trip'. I had misread the map or rather miscalculated the distances. But she was able positively to assure me, almost with a sense of triumph, that there were no Robin Goodwin pictures in the gallery. After drying out a little, she took on the most dire of jobs, what I call the 'death machine' – microfilms of all the people who died in England between 1977 and 1992 (when the parade ends). She was making an inventory of V. and S. Walls so that I could later check them out at the Family Records Centre in London to see if I could track down that portrait of a lady in a blue dress. We had not finished our work by the time the library closed that evening.

So we returned next morning to complete our lists and notes. Agnes May appeared to have spent her last ten years in Worthing. She arrived in late 1965 or early 1966 and lived in one of the maisonettes at The Towers, in Grand Avenue, West Worthing, to which we drove that afternoon. This is a tall, ornate building next to the front with fine views of the sea. It is a typical example of imposing sea-front architecture and looks expensive – probably too expensive for Agnes May who, after two or three years, moved to a less grand, red-brick apartment building, Downview Court in Boundary Road. These are small, comfortable 1930s flats with well-kept gardens but no sea views. After another two or three years, she moved again, this time to a more modest building of the same period, Arundel Court in Lansdowne Road, where she remained for the last four or five years of her life. All these buildings are in the same residential area of West Worthing, but each marks a step downwards. Her flat at Arundel Court is on the first floor (there is no lift) and has a narrow balcony facing east towards the town. It is adequate, but by no means luxurious. Agnes May was evidently in retreat.

At about the same time that she was moving into Arundel Court, Vera and Stephen Wall came to live in Pembroke Avenue a few hundred yards away. Since I had been unable to trace where they went after Agnes May's death, I decided to walk down Pembroke Avenue and, like a postman or milkman, knock at everyone's door. Dogs barked at me, curtains twitched and flapped, and I asked anyone brave enough to open the door if he or she knew Vera or Stephen Wall. No one did, but almost everyone thought that he or she knew someone who might – until I came full circle empty-handed. I stopped people in the street, went into banks, the Post Office, estate agents, undertakers, the crowded shopping centre nearby. Agnes May and Vera Wall had left no echo or rumour of themselves, no living memory.

After our two days in Worthing we drove back to London. For Maggie it had been a rather dreadful glimpse into the biographer's life – so banal and disappointing, the work, a mixture of arid drudgery in the library and pointless effrontery in the streets. What was the value of this raw, invasive questioning about ordinary people who never invited, let alone wanted, such persistent curiosity? Perhaps the motive behind this dogged pursuit, this hunt, was revenge against those who wounded my grandfather and my aunt. I felt slightly rattled by these speculations, believing my quest to be merely 'the proper study of mankind' – our appetite for discovery which is part of a natural curiosity about all life. But who can tell?

When we got back to London, Maggie ascended with relief into her fictional world (which uses researched facts as a runway into imaginative flight) and I went in search of Agnes May's half-length portrait in a blue dress. Because there are so many people with the name V. or S. Wall, it proved impossible to trace this picture through wills (I tried a dozen or so before submitting to this impossibility). I decided instead to find out more about the artist.

Robin Goodwin is an elusive painter, though his name is familiar to me. This is because, I remember, in the late 1940s he rented Augustus John's studio in Tite Street (John, having pocketed the money, continued to turn up at the studio causing much chaos and many mixed feelings). He had begun his professional career at the end of the Second World War, taught for a time at the Slade School of Fine Art, did commissioned portraits for the money and sea pictures for love. He appears to have exhibited everywhere, from the Royal Society of Marine Artists in Greenwich to the open-air shows along Victoria Embankment, but he joined none of the painters' societies, not even the Royal Society of Portrait Painters where he exhibited a number of his paintings. Among the list of his known portraits, none appear to be of Agnes May – she is unlikely to be the subject of *Sea Urchin*, *The Third Mate* (a woman) or even *Girl with a Fringe*. Robin Goodwin almost certainly painted Agnes May in Augustus John's studio in the late 1940s or early 1950s, after which time he turned increasingly to marine subjects. The portrait, which was probably commissioned by an admirer, is as much a signpost in her life as her Lalique glass, but I could not find where it pointed, its provenance or whereabouts.

Robin Goodwin died in 1999 aged ninety and his widow has no record of his portrait commissions. He is remembered best by his pupils, the most famous of whom, the successful animal painter David Shepherd, describes him as 'a fully qualified, hard-working sensible artist' who 'taught me to paint (if I had not met him I would be driving a bus)' and adds 'I owe him everything'. But among his sitters, David Shepherd cannot recall Agnes May. I contact several other painters whom he taught – among them one who reminds me that she held an exhibition of her work at Philippa Pullar's house in Barnes. Robin Goodwin, she confirms, was a very successful society portrait painter fifty years ago, and so it is not surprising that no one can identify this single sitter. Somewhere perhaps his unidentified oil painting, half-length, of a lady in blue dress still hangs, but I have run out of clues that might lead me to it.

So I switch my attention to the second picture, described in Agnes May's will as a 'water colour Portrait in silver frame'. This has been left to the third executor, Mrs Patricia Ellegard. How can I find her?

David Sutton knew the answer. It is www.192.com, a website called Info Disk. Its principal source material comes from the British Telecom directories and the local electoral registers throughout the United Kingdom, all loaded into a database which can be searched in a variety of ways. 'This is nothing more or less than helpful, publicly available information,' David assured me, 'but I am always a little uneasy when I recall that I first learnt about it from a radio programme about the likely *modus operandi* of Jill Dando's murderer.'

What I was looking for was simply an address to which I could write. Fortunately the surname Ellegard is extremely rare. David Sutton found her in less than ten minutes, living just outside London in the stockbroker suburbs of Middlesex – golf course and new town country.

Dear Mrs Ellegard,

I wonder if you could help me. I am very anxious to find out some information about the late Agnes May Beaumont-Thomas who died at Worthing towards the end of 1974. She was, earlier on, a close friend of my grandfather about whom I have been writing. I have never seen a photo of her, and her life after the 1940s is rather a mystery to me. I believe you knew her over these later years and would be very grateful for any help you could give me – perhaps (if it would not be inconvenient for you) I might pay you a short visit. In any event I very much look forward to hearing from you.

I ended the letter with an apology for writing out of the blue and troubling her in this way, posted it that evening, and waited.

I waited a week. Then Mrs Ellegard telephoned while I was out and left a message. She doubted whether she could give me much help. I could not ring her back because her number had not been disclosed. I recognised that this was a delicate matter and needed diplomacy. After another fortnight I wrote again, thanking her for ringing, asking her to telephone me again and giving her various times when I would be at home. She did ring again and I invited myself to tea, promising to bring her a copy of my family memoir. She was somewhat reluctant to see me, but what persuaded her was my understandable wish to see what my grandfather's friend, her friend too, looked like. She had a picture of her, she said – and I knew at once that this must be the 'water colour Portrait in silver frame' listed in Agnes May's will.

The following week I drove to Middlesex, arrived early, parked my car and looked around. This is a fairly expensive area of tree-lined avenues and squares, neo-houses with neat gardens, occupied, I imagine, by retiring, middle-class, successful businessmen and their families. I walk the streets until I can arrive at Mrs Ellegard's house at the polite hour. Then I ring the bell, speak into an entryphone, and stand there like a soldier. I hear the laborious sound of bolts being moved across and keys twisted: then the door opens.

Mrs Ellegard is a refined, rather nervous, white-haired lady probably in her late seventies. She lives alone in this well-protected house set in a quiet circle of differentiated yet similar houses, her husband, a 'hotel negotiator', having died three years ago (she points to his cheerful photograph in colour on the wall). I follow her into her drawing room and she offers me a cup of tea. But when I accept this offer, we find ourselves confronting the first of several difficulties that afternoon. How is she to deal with this tricky problem of tea? It is a rather awful complication. Should she leave me, a stranger, alone in the drawing room or take me with her into the kitchen, which is hardly the place for a man? Neither course strikes her as quite satisfactory, altogether correct. I consider cancelling the tea, but feel I cannot. We stand paralysed with sensitivity. Then I suggest that I can read her newspaper – a rather sensational tabloid I see lying on a chair – and sign the copy of my memoir which I have brought for her while she marshals the tea. In manly and ladylike fashions, we will, I point out, be simultaneously employed. Rather hesitantly she agrees to this solution and I am left to ponder the agonised negotiations ahead.

There are, I notice, no books in the room; nor can I see any of the items Agnes May bequeathed her friend – two silver swans, a sweet basket, the Lalique vase with thorns . . . It is a rather bare place, this room, painted hospital-white, spotlessly clean and extremely tidy – it shines with taste and the absence of life. There are a few plates on vertical display, a jug, one meagre plant on the window-sill above the discreet radiator. The atmosphere is that of a museum from which all objects of interest have been removed. What I see gives me few clues as to the owner's personality. The polished surfaces with large, immaculate spaces in between convey a sense of controlled anxiety.

Ten minutes later we are sitting at different sides of this room with our cups of tea and pieces of cake trying to make conversation. I hear myself parading my credentials. I mention the Royal Society of Literature and even my CBE. Why am I doing this? It is to establish my respectability and set my host's mind at rest. But my babbling is not noticeably successful. Mrs Ellegard may not read books, but she has an active imagination and entertains a very lively fear of the world outside her house – about which she must read each day in her newspaper. I have come from that fearful world outside and she feels apprehensive.

Our conversation over the next hour is stilted, but I do learn some interesting facts, and fantasies, about Agnes May. She had asked Mrs Ellegard to be one of her trustees and executors of her will because she had no family of her own, being a single child, and brought up in an orphanage. She had married once, nursed her husband when he contracted polio, and then been dreadfully hurt and shocked when he, an invalid, began an affaire with one of her friends. It did not seem natural or right. Until the 1940s, she had lived a very smart society life, but came down sadly in the world after separating from her husband, and would sometimes speak feelingly of her 'reduced circumstances' when Patricia first met her in the 1950s.

Patricia Ellegard cannot remember how they met, though it was before her own marriage. She does remember, however, being invited early in their friendship to tea in Agnes May's flat at Chelsea Cloisters in London, and being given strawberries. She had been impressed by those strawberries which were quite a rare luxury then (post-war food rationing having continued in Britain into the 1950s). 'Manita knew how to do things well,' she adds admiringly, still remembering the strawberries.

Manita is the name she gave Agnes May. Hearing her use it for the first time, the letters re-form in my mind and appear as 'Man-eater'. But of course I cannot say this. Patricia knew that some people called her 'Maimie', but she liked being called different names, new names, and this one, Manita, seemed for some reason to suit her. It stuck.

I ask her about Chelsea Cloisters and am told that Manita

had an admirer who lived there, a gentleman who would escort her to parties and take her out to dinner; but Mrs Ellegard cannot remember his name (and he is not mentioned in Agnes May's will).

Our conversation stops, and I try to get it going by asking some innocuous questions. Why did Agnes May leave London? Mrs Ellegard tells me that she went to Worthing to be near her ex-husband in Brighton, Mr Beaumont-Thomas, with whom she hoped to be reunited. The fact was she was not sensible with money. The clouds were darkening, but she had not saved for a rainy day and by the mid-1960s could no longer afford her carefree strawberry life in Chelsea.

The conversation stops again. And starts again. Patricia Ellegard (or Patsy, as she was called) used to go down occasionally to Worthing where she met Manita's new friends and fellow executors, the solicitor and the Wall family, Vera and Stephen. She did not like them – and they did not like one another. The solicitor was a 'creepy' man who she felt had never looked after Manita's financial affairs as he should have done, though they saw a good deal of each other. As for Vera Wall, she found it difficult to understand what Manita saw in her. She was a nondescript, rather common woman in her late fifties, perhaps older, who worked in the Post Office, and was probably too interested in Manita's money – what was left of it. As for Stephen Wall, he was taken out of Manita's will because she felt he was being too friendly. Perhaps he wanted the Wall family to get all her money – in any event something had gone wrong between them, though not with Vera Wall. She stayed, like a limpet. On one occasion Mrs Ellegard took her husband Neil down to Worthing to give Manita some financial advice after Mr Beaumont-Thomas had settled extra money on her, but when they arrived they found that she had already blown a good deal of it on an expensive fur coat. That was very typical of her.

We stop and start again. Usually Mrs Ellegard travelled to Worthing by herself. Manita, who owned a small car, would meet her at the station and take her to her club. 'I will introduce you as my niece,' she rather mysteriously volunteered on her first visit, and this pretence was kept up, though there were very few of these introductions. Manita appeared to be leading a reserved and isolated life, almost secret, without real friends or family, and to be suffering from some anxiety. In the last year or two, when she became ill with a heart condition, Mrs Ellegard did not see her at all. Whenever she telephoned, Vera Wall would answer – it was very off-putting. She did not go to her friend's funeral either, because the solicitor discouraged her from doing so. In her opinion, Manita had fallen into very bad company at Worthing. It was not surprising that, though she was really a vulnerable and sensitive woman, her contact with the world had also made her hard – that was, very critical of people, especially men.

This story has come out in bits and pieces, and now there is no more that Patricia Ellegard can tell me. So I ask her about the picture – the 'water colour Portrait in silver frame in my lounge' – that Agnes May had given her. It has been in Mrs Ellegard's cupboard for the best part of twenty-five years, but she has kindly found it, dusted it, in preparation for my arrival, and now brings it into the drawing room and places it in an armchair. So, for the first time, I see my grandfather's secret mistress, for whom he left home and almost, with the aid of many lawyers, bankrupted the family.

My first reaction is one of bewilderment. What am I looking at? Is it really a watercolour? It seems more like a coloured photograph. It is not large, about 60 by 25 centimetres, I estimate, within its silver frame. But I have no doubt that I am looking at an accurate representation of Agnes May. She is aged, I would say, about thirty – in her early thirties anyway – which is the time my grandfather knew her. She wears a soft, draped, floral-print dress of silk crêpe-de-chine. Her hands are raised as if in prayer – not quite prayer – on second thoughts the gesture is rather more winsome, almost flirtatious though not immodest, and her head is cocked slightly to one side as she eyes the artist/cameraman with a slight smile. In the lower right-hand corner there is a signature in what appears to be pencil. Mrs Ellegard and I approach the picture together, crouch and bend before it as if it were a religious icon, and try to decipher the name. 'Janet' is fairly clear, but the second name is more difficult to read – it may, we agree, be 'Evans'.

We move back and begin our negotiations. I ask whether I may borrow the picture for a few days, have a reproduction made, and return it to her within the week. But Mrs Ellegard says she would rather not do this. I ask whether, at my expense, she would hire a professional photographer herself to make a copy for me. But Mrs Ellegard replies that she would prefer to photograph it herself and, to close the matter, she goes to get her camera and, trying to avoid reflections from the glass, she begins snapping it at various distances from the chair. The film in her camera is fairly new and it will be several weeks, she informs me, before she can have the negative developed. 'I must not keep you any longer,' she suddenly announces, ushering me to the door. I have obviously delighted her enough. Outside again, I hear the bolts and keys being manoeuvred with a sense of relief, and I walk back to my car.

I sit in the car making notes on what Mrs Ellegard has said, and reflect on the implications. She has not thought to reveal much, partly because she is on her guard (she might have spoken more easily to another woman – as Patsy and Manita probably spoke together) and partly because she is not given to analysing character and describing details (she cannot recall the oil painting left to Vera Wall). Much of what she has told me of Manita/Agnes May might, equally, I think, apply to herself, though she has been more cautious in her life – her drawing room is a monument to caution. She exudes an aroma of respectability, but beneath the acquired cultivation of her voice runs an insinuation of scandal and unsavouriness – the sort of drama she must spy, as though a periscope, when reading her newspaper. She has conjured up in my mind a picture of Agnes May at the centre of a small gang of people continually at odds with one another, like a trio or quartet which cannot find the right pitch or tempi. I begin to see them as aspects of Agnes May's own character

273

which, for ever inharmonious, has carried her to this lonely and insecure conclusion of her life. Patricia Ellegard represents a younger version of herself. She must have been pretty when young, upwardly mobile like Agnes May herself, but, whatever adventures she may have had, she steered her way skilfully through the hazards. She has come through. Agnes May could well have relived something of her youth in Patricia's company even if she could not learn from her carefulness how to play her cards better. She needed men around her who were married, who could give her reassurance, protection and the prospect of a good life, men who knew the male world of business. But there had to be a sexual ingredient in her relationship with men, even if it was only in play, and she could not really make friends with them since instinctively she was always making use of them. Even in her late seventies she dyed her white hair blonde and, as Mrs Ellegard hinted, she may well have flirted with Stephen Wall. Perhaps she was at her most natural with Vera Wall, who was nearer her age than Patricia Ellegard and whose class appears to have been similar to Agnes May's origins. There was no need to pretend that she was a niece or any other relation, no call to take her to the smart club in Worthing. She could relax and be her old self. Vera looked after her almost like a domestic servant (like the domestic servant at the Bickerstaff home when she was young). This is how I interpret what I have been told.

While waiting for Mrs Ellegard to send me the photograph of Agnes May, I followed some of the leads she had given me. First of all I went to the Chelsea Reference

Library in the King's Road and examined in the street directory the lists of tenants living at Chelsea Cloisters. Agnes May appears to have moved there in 1947 and for a couple of years she had two addresses – her apartment at Ennismore Gardens in Knightsbridge as well as flat number 637 in Chelsea Cloisters. By 1951 she has given up Ennismore Gardens and transferred to flat number 911 on the top floor of Chelsea Cloisters where her new friend Patricia comes to tea.

I know Chelsea Cloisters. It is some three hundred yards from Sloane Avenue Mansions where my mother lived between husbands in the late 1940s and even nearer to Nell Gwynn House, the block of flats where I wrote my first book in the late 1950s. I must surely have passed Agnes May in the street during the years we lived so close to each other. It is a tantalising thought.

Could there be anyone there now who remembers Agnes May? I find one tenant, a legend in the building, who has been there almost fifty years. He is eager to help. Yes, he remembers her vividly – he is almost sure he does. Isn't she the woman who was so often at Buckingham Palace? His voice cracks with amusement, with excitement. A lady-in-waiting, that's what she was, sparkling with evening jewels. What else would I like to hear? What would please me? We float in this dreamland until we are out of breath, when I fall back to earth and try to find a more solid trail of research.

Chelsea Cloisters, built in red brick during the late 1930s, is one of four large, rather forbidding but comfortable, private blocks of flats between the King's Road and Fulham Road in Sloane Avenue. It was known in the 1950s for its artist tenants, most particularly Matthew Smith, and it seems likely that it was during her early days here, probably commissioned by her gentleman admirer, that Agnes May had her portrait painted nearby in Tite Street. Robin Goodwin, unlike Augustus John, preferred middle-aged to very young sitters. This oil painting was clearly a more substantial work than the modest, silver-framed rather mysterious picture I had seen at Mrs Ellegard's house, but it must have shown Agnes May some twenty-five years after my grandfather knew her. For my purpose, the 'water colour in silver frame' is the portrait I want, and after two months of waiting I grew anxious as to whether I would ever see it again.

In early December Mrs Ellegard sent me a tasteful Christmas card and, my hopes rising, I immediately sent a card decorated with suggestive angels to her. Another month went by and my hopes began to sink once more. Then, in January, she sent me the fruits of her camerawork. Only one photograph had come out at all reasonably, but it was small and not perfectly in focus. I was immensely relieved yet slightly disappointed, and decided to write to Mrs Ellegard and argue my case for a professional reproduction.

Dear Mrs Ellegard,
    I really am most grateful to you for seeing me, answering my questions, and taking these photographs. It was kind of you.

I immediately took your photos to see if they could be professionally enlarged . . . [but] though it is a very good amateur photograph of what is evidently a charming watercolour, I was told it would 'not meet reproduction standards'. This puts me in some difficulty. I am very conscious of disturbing you and have no wish to intrude. On the other hand, here is an artist's portrait that was painted to be seen – and would do no one any harm by being seen. It is my belief that Agnes May would not have kept this portrait if she had disliked it . . . I therefore have to ask whether you would mind having it professionally reproduced at my expense . . . The larger oil painting which was left to Vera Wall has been lost – and I consider this a great shame and not what was intended when it was left to her. You have the only likeness of Agnes May in her younger years.

In her reply, Mrs Ellegard wrote that 'during the few years of my friendship with Agnes May Beaumont-Thomas, I found her to be a rather private and sensitive person'. The disclosure of her liaison with my grandfather, she continued, 'which was of a relative short period of time, in her early life, would have caused her great distress'. Therefore, she concluded, while happy to let me have her snapshots, she was unwilling to provide any further help that might compromise her friend's privacy.

All biographers will be familiar with these sentiments, and many readers may find themselves in agreement. These feelings are natural and go deep. But I maintain that it is the privacy of the living that should be protected, while the dead no longer require it, cannot be distressed by it, are above it. They can still, however, contribute through their posthumous disclosures to our understanding of the living world.

I was sure that Mrs Ellegard would not change her mind, but felt I must make one more appeal. So I wrote again, explaining that I was not seeking scandalous gossip, not attacking the privacy of Agnes May's late years, simply trying to obtain the best possible likeness of her in her youth. 'An artist painted her portrait,' I wrote, 'she sat for it. You have had it for many years in a cupboard which has helped to preserve its freshness. But may I suggest, without any disrespect, that this is taking privacy too far? I believe it deserves to be seen – that is why it was painted – that is why Agnes May kept it. When one receives a gift from a friend like this, one also receives a responsibility. One day, if we are not careful, no one will know who it is.'

I noticed a slightly pompous, bullying tone beginning to enter my letter, and sought to soften this by offering to show Mrs Ellegard anything I might eventually write about Agnes May. Then I signed off with an apology for invading her own privacy. To this letter I never received an answer.

So I had to content myself with investigating what I had. Mrs Ellegard remembered that Agnes May had told her the artist 'was highly thought of and much in demand during the 1920s'. But nowhere could I find a watercolourist or photographer named Janet Evans, and nor could the curator of the Twentieth Century Collection at the National Portrait Gallery, Honor Clerk. I had worked with her before on exhibitions at the gallery and she had recently helped me with my search for the elusive Robin Goodwin. She is an encyclopaedia of knowledge, and if she had never heard of Janet Evans then I felt confident that no such professional photographer existed. For, having shown Mrs Ellegard's snapshot to several experts, I was now convinced that this portrait was a hand-painted or overpainted version of a studio photograph.

Honor Clerk has not merely encyclopaedic knowledge, she is an ingenious lateral thinker, and soon came up with a new idea. In the mid-1920s, she told me, a camerawoman called Peg Jevons defected from Dorothy Wilding's celebrated photographic studio and set up in business with another woman photographer, Janet Tyrell, creating a firm in Mayfair named Janet Jevons. There are a dozen or so of their prints in the National Portrait Gallery, and I examine the signatures on the lower right-hand corner. I recognise them at once as the same signature before which Mrs Ellegard and I bowed down in her drawing room before intoning the wrong name. The Janet Jevons studio was very close to the apartment in Piccadilly which my grandfather bought for Agnes May, and I have no doubt that this picture, showing what she looked like soon after they met, was his gift to her. This is an accurate portrait and a memento of the woman for whom my grandfather left home.

Agnes May was to enjoy another twenty years of high

living after this likeness was made and before the downward spiral of her life began. Then, over a further twenty years or more, a slow decline: from Knightsbridge into Chelsea, and from London off to Worthing, one of the most genteel of English seaside resorts. She would achieve some spirited moments during this retreat – the oil portrait painted in Augustus John's old studio surely marking one of them. Even in her early seventies she was making a dramatic stand, accompanied by her solicitor on the steps of the High Court, waving a doctor's certificate as she intervened in a case which her husband, Reggie Beaumont-Thomas, was bringing to Chancery – had been bringing to Chancery for the last several years.*

---

*Soon after the Variation of Trusts Act 1958 became law the Beaumont-Thomas family hatched a scheme to reduce the duty to be paid on the Trusts set up in the will of Reggie's father. The plan, which involved Agnes May as a 'reversionary annuitant', required Reggie to take out an insurance policy against his death.

The case was barely in its sixth or eighth year when Agnes May, claiming that the anxiety of waiting was making her ill, staged her dramatic intervention 'with the result that we heard on Monday that the case was coming on today [18 July 1967]', wrote one of the platoon of solicitors, insurance agents, actuaries and impecunious beneficiaries. 'This took us completely by surprise . . . I would like to say that this is the end of the matter, but unfortunately it is not, because at the last minute the Order that we were asking for had to be varied because of a condition made by Mrs Beaumont-Thomas . . . now we have to go back to the Court of Protection.'

Eventually Agnes May received a lump sum of £6,000 plus an annual income of £2,000 which was to continue until her death even if Reggie

She was to die of heart failure at the Berkeley Lodge Nursing and Convalescent Home, next to Worthing Hospital, on 12 December 1974. The instructions in her will were clear. 'I desire that there should be no mourners and no flowers.' There was little to celebrate now and she must have dreaded the possibility of so many contradictory parts of her life coming together at her death: the Bickerstaffs and Beaumont-Thomases, her sisters' and

---

died first – all this (in addition to the settlement Reggie had made) came from the will of a father-in-law whom she never met and who had died almost twenty years before her marriage to his son.

The significance of this to me is it suggests that had the Holroyd family discovered the Variation of Trusts Act 1958, it might have broken their own ruinous family Trust set up by my grandfather to secure funds for his family after he absconded with Agnes May (a trust that in due course almost bankrupted the family).

Despite his ill-health, Reggie Beaumont-Thomas outlived Agnes May. He died at Brighton in 1981 leaving approximately £650,000, a rather trivial sum by his family's standards. But part of his plan had been to ensure that his common-law wife Vera Thomas had enough money following his death. In this he appears to have been successful. On her death in 1991 she left a respectable two and a half million pounds.

One curious happening which arose following Reggie's death was the reappearance of his first wife, the Parisian dancing girl Germaine Blanche Aimée Dubor from whom he had been divorced in 1933. The French government instituted proceedings to have the annuity Reggie had been paying her for the past fifty years continued after his death and paid out of his estate. This ingeniously argued case eventually failed, and the French government was obliged to pay for her care in a home.

husband's families – and even, a final horror, her previous husbands.*

Nor did she want a gravestone to perpetuate and repeat her names and dates: her stories with their many beginnings and endings. At the very end she seems to have wanted simply to make what haste she could and be gone. 'I desire that my body may be cremated and my ashes scattered.' While Vera Wall cleared out her flat at Arundel Court (which mysteriously remained empty for several years), the solicitor took charge of the ashes. But no one now knows where they were deposited or released into the air.

Somewhere perhaps, hanging in someone's home or at a gallery, an oil painting 'half-length Portrait of a Lady in blue dress', still exists. It will have Robin Goodwin's signature on it, but no mention of the sitter who, in middle age, has finally lost her identity as she always wished to do, though without

---

* Though she almost certainly did not know this, her first two husbands had married again and were dead. William Lisle, who had informed Agnes May that his father was a solicitor (he was actually a clerk in a solicitor's office) and that he was a man of money, an accountant (though he too was a solicitor's clerk), married Lily Matthews, the daughter of a postmaster, in 1924 and died in 1936 leaving £450. Thomas Babb worked for a short time as an electrical engineer in the same Royal Air Force office as Henry Haselhurst and was awarded the CBE. He married a divorcée, Marie Louise Welter (née Vermière) in 1934 but, like Agnes May, she left him. He went back to live with his mother for several years in Minehead and died in 1957 only two or three miles from my father and aunt in Surrey, looked after by a lady from London. His mother's estate had been valued in 1951 at approximately £10,000, but he left only £800 six years later.

gaining another permanent name or recognition for herself.

But I have the reproduction of the hand-coloured photograph, originally commissioned by my grandfather. I have had it enhanced and have restored her name to it. For nearly a quarter of a century it has lain in the dark. This is Agnes May in her adult prime, as she appeared soon after my grandfather met her during the General Strike of 1926, the woman who serenaded him from home, setting off all manner of emotional and financial shock waves that ended seventy years later with my aunt and myself.

I feel my quest is over. I have found her. She is here.

The Beaumont-Thomas Family

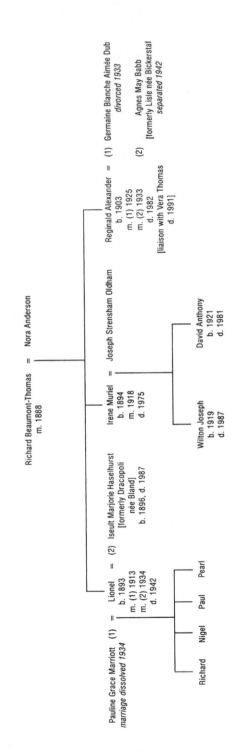

Richard Beaumont-Thomas = Nora Anderson
m. 1888

Pauline Grace Marriott (1) = Lionel = (2) Iseult Marjorie Haselhurst
marriage dissolved 1934   b. 1893   [formerly Dracopoli]
                              m. (1) 1913   née Bland]
                              m. (2) 1934   b. 1896, d. 1987
                              d. 1942

Richard   Nigel   Paul   Pearl

Irene Muriel = Joseph Strensham Oldham
b. 1894
m. 1918
d. 1975

Wilton Joseph   David Anthony
b. 1919   b. 1921
d. 1987   d. 1981

Reginald Alexander = (1) Germaine Blanche Aimée Dub
b. 1903   *divorced 1933*
m. (1) 1925
m. (2) 1933   (2) Agnes May Babb
d. 1982   [formerly Lisle née Bickerstaf
[liaison with Vera Thomas   *separated 1942*
d. 1991]

The Haselhurst Family

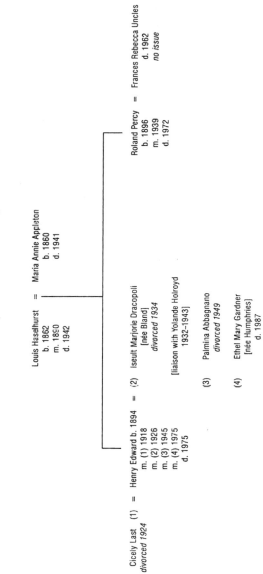

Louis Haselhurst = Maria Annie Appleton
b. 1862   b. 1860
m. 1890   d. 1941
d. 1942

Cicely Last (1) = Henry Edward b. 1894 = (2) Iseult Marjorie Dracopoli   Roland Percy = Frances Rebecca Uncles
divorced 1924   m. (1) 1918   [née Bland]   b. 1896   d. 1962
                   m. (2) 1926   *divorced 1934*   m. 1939   *no issue*
                   m. (3) 1945   d. 1972
                   m. (4) 1975   [liaison with Yolande Holroyd
                   d. 1975   1932–1943]

                                    (3) Palmina Abbagnano
                                         divorced 1949

                                    (4) Ethel Mary Gardner
                                         [née Humphries]
                                         d. 1987

The Bickerstaff Family

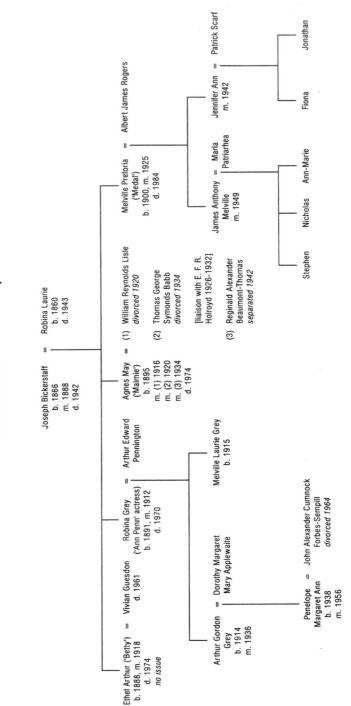

The Holroyd Family

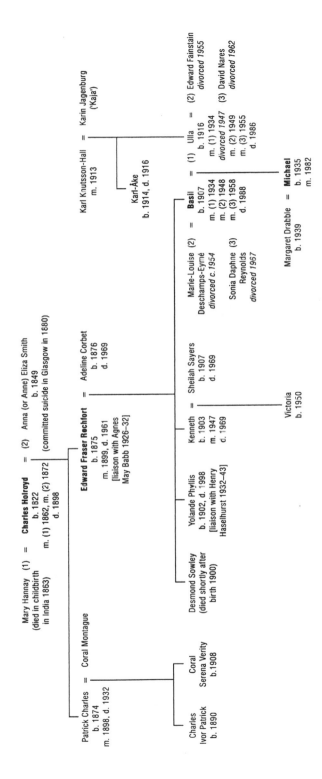